THE Flourishing LIFE

Discovering the transforming power of trusting God with your weaknesses, ways and wants

STEPHANIE BEAULIEU

Video sessions were made possible by a generous partnership with CNBC Women.

Since I became a Christian as a young adult, I have loved women's Bible study. God first laid an idea on my heart years ago. While on a plane to Calgary from Winnipeg, I was reading my Bible, praying and considering all the changes in my life. I was overwhelmed with thankfulness to God, and so grateful for the transforming power of His Word. As I was reflecting on women I knew, a thought came to my mind: "Just the Word." If all women, everywhere, could just get into the Word, they could be transformed. One of the values of the Canadian National Baptist Convention is "all kinds of churches for all kinds of people." We are pleased to partner with Stephanie and offer you this bite-size Bible study, an opportunity to get into the Word in small, bite-size chunks. I look forward to seeing women connect with the Word and hearing how God uses His Word to transform lives!

Kathy Morales
CNBC Women's Ministry Leader

cnbc women

To learn more, visit http://www.cnbc.ca

ISBN 978-1-9995601-3-3

Printed and bound at Supreme Printing Ltd. in Calgary, Alberta, Canada

Cover photo by oksix from Getty Images Pro.

Table of Contents

About the Author

Stephanie Morales-Beaulieu is a lover and communicator of God's Word and shares that passion online, from the stage, in her living room and anywhere else God opens a door. Bite-size Bible study was birthed out of a heart and a passion to make the transforming power of the Word accessible to those new to Scripture, those overwhelmed by it, and those longing to be transformed by it.

She has authored three bite-size Bible studies including *A Roadmap to Trials* (2014), *Walk in Love* (2016) and, most recently, *The Flourishing Life* (2019). She is a born communicator with contagious love and enthusiasm for Jesus. As a wife to Mike and mom to Sophie, Jonah and Eli, she shares from her wealth of relatable stories that will inspire you to see everyday life through the lens of truth. She is authentic and funny, and you will wish she lived next door.

Dedicated to my tribe...

They say it takes a village to raise a child. It also takes a tribe to birth a Bible study. What you're holding in your hand right now would not have been possible without the collective effort of an army.

Michaela, Jessie, Emily and Carolyn: Thank you for combing through the content as I created it over those initial 40 days. You brought each of your strengths—clarity, brevity, encouragement and questions, and you made it richer. Jessie, the day that God laid it on my heart to create a finished product like this one, you texted me and shared how you still thought about trusting God with your weaknesses, ways and wants. It was fuel for that step of faith that day. Carolyn—you took a mountain of content and beautifully refined it. Your edits, suggestions, and eye for detail made it into something I couldn't have. Thank you for your patience and faithfulness throughout the process, and we both know it was a process! Derick and Marielle, for selflessly and generously giving of your time to shoot, reshoot and produce the videos. Connie, for encouraging me and praying me through without an ounce of condemnation each time it took longer than I hoped. My army of prayer warriors who cover and carry me as I seek to fulfill the call God has placed on my life to spread the Word. Mom, for always desiring to fan into flame the gifts of God you've seen in me and having a heart to see women transformed by the Word. CNBC Women, thank you for your willingness to invest in the kingdom in this way. Katelyn—for speaking truth over my brokenness and tears the day I was certain it would never get done and celebrating when I crossed the finish line. Sam, for taking a step of faith and leading the launch team, so this message of flourishing could get into the hands and hearts of women everywhere. Lola, thank you for your investment with the kids and love for them that gifted me this time. Mike, my constant champion and encourager, I hardly have words for how your love has revealed to me the heart of God. And to Jesus, my Lord and Saviour, the One who constantly invites me deeper, knowing You is worth more than gold. Thank You for calling me out of functioning into flourishing.

Start Here:

This bite-size Bible study has two parts: the personal study guide that you're holding in your hands, and five video sessions. To access the videos, please visit:

http://everydaytruth.ca/flourish

You will receive video session 1 immediately following email sign up. After that, one video per week will be sent to you automatically.

What should I expect?

In the same way our bodies need physical food regularly, our Spirits need the nourishment of God's Word. This guide is designed for daily use to help you access that spiritual nourishment for 28 days. Each day consists of these sections designed to work through in 15 to 30 minutes.

Read it:

Scriptures from the Parable of the Sower and other related verses.

Unpack it:

Questions to help you comprehend what you've read.

Work it out:

Stories and reflection questions to help you understand how it applies to your life.

Talk to God about it:

A framework to help you converse with God (taken from the Lord's prayer) about what He's revealed to you about Himself (HE), what He's revealing about you (ME), and an invitation to ask the Holy Spirit what you want Him to do in and through you (WE).

Answer the questions as if He's sitting across from you gently probing your heart and mind, asking you to take an honest inventory of what you find, and trusting that while some things may be a surprise to you, they never are to Him. Resist the urge to rush through the last part and remember that conversing with a person involves both sharing and listening. When you don't know what to say to Him, ask Him to speak, and then simply respond. Seek to stay connected to His Holy Spirit throughout the day, with the same priority you give staying connected to your phone.

The last day of each week of study is a reflection day to look back and intentionally remember what God has been teaching you. This will serve as a bridge to the video sessions, which practically explore the material in a way that will help you live it out.

Who should I do this study with?

You can do this study on your own, but since God created us for community, I strongly recommend inviting at least two friends along for the journey. Change happens as we are honest with God, others, and ourselves. Share what you're learning, cheer each other on, and pick each other up when you fall. Ask God to bring people to mind and then simply extend an invite, link arms, and do the study together. Friends flourish together.

Gather your study materials and keep them in the place that you will spend your time alone with God each day. I would encourage you to have a hard copy of the Bible, a bookmark, a pen, pencil and highlighter to accompany your personal study guide. Make a daily appointment with God and commit to it much like you would a meeting on your calendar. And if you miss it, receive the grace to try again tomorrow.

First steps:

1. Watch Video Session 1 (an introduction to the study) and complete the discussion/reflection questions individually, with a friend or small group.
2. Complete the activities each day for Week 1 of personal study.
3. Move on to Week 2 and repeat.

Introduction to the Flourishing Life

A couple of years ago, I posed a question to my women's small group: *What is something that has recently changed your life? Tell the person next to you about it."* With ease and excitement, they buzzed about how Amazon Prime had transformed their shopping experience, click and collect had taken the stress out of buying groceries and packing cubes had brought much needed order to the chaos that formerly ruled in their suitcases while travelling.

Transformation is easy to talk about because we're simply testifying to our experiences. A clear problem was overcome by a clear solution. What is clear to us is easy to communicate to others.

My next sentence was, "*Now turn and share the gospel with that same person.*"

Only crickets could be heard.

What are we missing when it comes to Jesus? Our minds are informed. We know what the Bible says and that it's good news. We know the eternal trajectories of our lives have been changed, but perhaps we're not always certain of how Jesus transforms our everyday lives.

We can't talk about the Gospel with ease, excitement and clarity when we're still wrestling with questions and realities such as "Why don't I feel different?" or "Why do I feel stuck?" or "Why can't I seem to change?" or "Why does my mind know so much more than my heart has experienced?"

When sharing the good news, I used to secretly think, "I don't sound very convincing." I sounded like I was sharing theoretical information about Jesus rather than transformational experience. **Information doesn't compel people the same way transformation does.**

The noticeable gap between what the Bible says about the life Jesus came to give me and what I had experienced led me to conclude, "There has got to be more than this."

God took that cry of my heart as an invitation to take me on a surprising journey, not of adding more to my life but of giving Him more of me. He gently broke me open and started digging to reveal the hardened, shallow and crowded places in my heart. As I studied the parable of the Sower, He began to reveal that what I had believed were obstacles to intimacy with Him were actually opportunities to trust Him. And this is where transformation began to take place.

The flourishing life is characterized by spiritual fruitfulness and kingdom productivity, but not as a result of our performance. It rests in the depth of our connection to God. More depth obviously requires going deeper, and going deeper begins with breaking ground.

Our job isn't to create the crop or manufacture the fruit. Fruit *happens* in good soil. Our goal is to *take responsibility to relentlessly prepare* our hearts for His use and *relinquish the results* to Him. We focus on the field, not the yield. Soil serves a specific purpose—it is simply the *environment* where seed sown can flourish into fruit grown.

Flourishing isn't about trying harder or doing better, but simply surrendering at every turn and making more room for Jesus to be at home in our hearts.

My prayer is that you will flourish as you invite God to dig deep into your heart so you become deeply rooted and grounded in His love, filled with the fullness of God, and that He will overflow from your life in ways that will transform eternity.

Let's get started! I'm so humbled and thankful to be on this journey with you,

Stephanie

Video session 1 is available at http://everydaytruth.ca/flourish

Session 1: A New Pattern

Matthew 13:1–9, Ephesians 3:16–19

In survival mode we ________________ , but when we're thriving, we ______________________

FLOURISHING: 1: growing ________________: THRIVE; to be in a state of activity or production; growing or developing in a healthy or _________________________ way; especially as a result of a __________________________ environment;

1. To flourish, we must _____________ _____________.

   This isn't about ______________, it's about _________________.

2. To flourish, _____________ _____________.

3. To flourish, _____________.

4. To flourish, _____________.

Session 1 Reflection/Discussion Questions:

1. What drew you to *The Flourishing Life*?

2. Would you describe your current state as surviving or thriving? What factors would you identify as contributing?

3. How do you feel when you consider going for depth rather than width? What comes to mind when you consider giving God more square footage in your heart?

4. Have you thought of maturity in Christ as a point you'll one day reach, or a constant state of staying with Him? What do you think now?

5. What do you sense God is speaking to you about right now?

The Path

Day 1: Packed Down Places

Read it:

[3] Then he told them many things in parables, saying: "Consider the sower who went out to
sow. [4] As he sowed, some seed fell along the path, and the birds came and devoured them"
(Matt. 13:3–4).

[18] "So listen to the parable of the sower: [19] When anyone hears the word about the kingdom and
doesn't understand it, the evil one comes and snatches away what was sown in his heart. This is
the one sown along the path" (Matt. 13:18–19).

[5]Then He got into the boat with them, and the wind ceased. They were completely astounded,
because they had not understood about the loaves. Instead, their hearts were hardened (Mark
6:51–52).

Unpack it:

- Underline what the seed is compared to (Matt. 13:19).
- Circle what happens when the word is sown along the path (Matt. 13:19).
- Put brackets around the result of not understanding (Matt. 13:19).
- Underline the four words that describe what kept the disciples from understanding (Mark 6:52).

Work it out:

My backyard is home to a small garden box with space for a few rows of seed. After bearing the weight of winter, the hardened soil must be tilled if it is to be used. Unless the soil is broken open, seeds will simply sit on top of the hardened surface where they have no chance of taking root or bearing fruit.

At times, I have felt this way—as if the truth is sitting on top of my heart rather than taking root and bearing fruit. From there is simply informs my mind rather than transforms my heart. Here, sitting on top, it can be easily snatched away.

Today's Scripture revealed that our hearts can be hardened by a lack of understanding.

The word "understanding," from the Greek ***sunemi***, means: *from "sun" (together with) and "hiemi" (to send or put; to bring together).*

Sunemi means to *"put it all together and make sense out of it". It strictly denotes the collecting together of the single features of an object into a whole, as collecting the pieces of a puzzle and putting them together.*

Without understanding, we do not make sense of how desperately our hearts need to be transformed by truth. And if we do, we don't know how.

Thankfully, according to Jesus, understanding isn't something we can simply go and get; it must be given.[1]

It can open the road between an informed mind and a transformed heart, but a hardened heart can be the barricade that keeps it closed.

1. What truths about God do you know in your head, but suspect have not yet made it to your heart? (The truths you feel informed about, but not yet transformed by may be a helpful starting point. If you aren't sure, ask the Holy Spirit to reveal.)

A hardened heart is defined as "*covered with a thick skin, or by covering with a callus.*"[2] Unlike blisters, which are caused by painful rubbing that is impossible to ignore, calluses often form *silently and without notable pain*. The thick and hardened skin results from ongoing friction. In the same way, spiritual hearts can harden subtly and silently over time.

What fuels the ongoing friction our hearts respond to? Fear.

Our hearts continually wonder about the answers to these defining questions—*Am I loved? Am I valuable? Am I enough?*

When our fear, guilt or shame answers rather than truth, we forge paths.

[1] Matthew 13:11.
[2] *Strong's*, G4456, "poroo," https://www.blueletterbible.org/lang/lexicon/lexicon.cfm?Strongs=G4456&t=KJV.

Perhaps early on you learned an automatic response to fear in the form of a pattern. Maybe it felt safe to erect self-protective walls around the fear of being unlovable. Or maybe your response to the fear of not being valuable was pride—to be okay on your own and never need another person.

In the same way that physical paths form, the soil of our hearts hardens as it is continuously packed down and tracked over by our answers to these questions. We are all afraid of something, even if we are unwilling to admit it, even to ourselves. Fear of failing, missing out, not being enough, being too much, not doing enough, and being rejected is continually pressing on and hardening our hearts.

2. Can you identify ways you have responded to fear, guilt, or shame in your own life? How well have those attempts worked to quiet your fears?

3. How might these attempts and resulting answers hindered God's truth from penetrating and transforming your heart?

Fear, guilt and shame fuel our patterns, self-protectiveness and pride, causing our hearts to slowly, subtly and surely harden over time. Over the next few days, we will unpack these a bit more but for today, take some time to reflect and respond. As you dialogue with God, ask Him to reveal what is hidden, break what is hardened, and to open your mind so you can understand Scripture.

There is no intimacy with God apart from interaction with Him.

"The Lord is gracious and compassionate, slow to anger, and rich in love. The Lord is good to all; he has compassion on all he has made" (Ps. 145:8–9).

Respond to Him about what He's revealed to you today.

Since it's our first day together, I've given you an example of what this time with the Lord might look like. Resist the temptation to speed through it. Express your heart to Him and listen for His.

Talk to God about it:

He: What has God revealed to you about Himself? Praise, thank or tell Him in the space below.

God, thank you that are truth and you give truth. Your word says you are gracious, compassionate, slow to anger, rich in love and good to all. I praise you for your unchanging character and the assurance you've given me in your Word of what you are like.

Your turn:

Me: What has He revealed to you about yourself? What do you need Him to give you, forgive you for or deliver you from? Tell Him in the space below.

You've shown me that I still stubbornly return to my own patterns and it's costly. Make me more sensitive to your Spirit on this journey so you can show me where I need you most. Forgive me for plunging ahead without asking you what is true. Deliver me from the evil one— from his distractions, from feeling overwhelmed which makes me want to quit, and my defaults that cause me to unplug from your Spirit.

Your turn:

We: What do you want Him to do in and through your life by the power of His Spirit? Ask Him here.

Reveal the ways that I'm currently responding to fear, guilt and shame. Show me my patterns, protective walls and pride that keep me from understanding truth. I want you to so transform my life that people see you in me and are drawn to Jesus. Fill me with more of you. I want to grow in a healthy way that shows other how you can make a person flourish from the inside out. Reveal: what makes it difficult for me to trust and surrender.

Your turn:

Day 2: That Thing You Do

Read it:

18 For I know that nothing good dwells in me, that is, in my flesh. For I have the desire to do what is right, but not the ability to carry it out. 19 For I do not do the good I want, but the evil I do not want is what I keep on doing. 20 Now if I do what I do not want, it is no longer I who do it, but sin that dwells within me (Rom. 7:18–20).

24 What a wretched man I am! Who will rescue me from this body of death? 25 Thanks be to God through Jesus Christ our Lord! So then, with my mind I myself am serving the law of God, but with my flesh, the law of sin (Rom. 7:24–25).

Unpack it:

- Underline what lives in us and circle the word that describes our ability to do good (Rom. 7:18).
- Put brackets around what we often find ourselves doing (Rom. 7:19).
- Circle what is at work in us (v. 20) and the name of the One who rescues us (Rom. 7:25).

Work it out:

It was a regular morning walk on a familiar path when a friend casually asked, "Why do you always do so much?" The question caught me off guard, and within seconds, I realized I didn't have an answer. I had always assumed that "doing so much" in the form of crushing to-do lists and tucking accomplishments under my belt was to be celebrated. I had never stopped to consider if there was another force driving me.

Have you ever wondered why you do that thing you do? If you were to look closely and deeply, what patterns might you find? There are patterns in the way we respond to the fear, guilt and shame that presses on our hearts. There are patterns in the way we answer questions about our worth, ability and significance, and in the way we respond to worry, stress, conflict, boredom, and feeling overwhelmed.

Repeatedly tracking over the same patterns packs down the soil of our hearts into hardened paths.

My own patterns flew under the radar of my consciousness for most of my life—patterns triggered by fear of failure and shame of feeling like I was never enough. I would strive to stick to the tasks and relationships that I was certain God called me to, but when I felt overwhelmed, I would hide in a distraction of choice. Have you ever done the same?

Striving can take many forms. We think the problem we haven't been able to solve or the habit we haven't been able to change remains simply because we haven't tried hard enough yet. So, we listen to the voice of the accuser who attempts to boss us around. *Keep busy. Keep everyone happy. Don't miss out. Stay in control. Do better. Be in the know. Work harder. Be perfect. Try more. Most of all, don't fail.* So, we work. We do more. We control. We accomplish. We make lists and set goals. These are not inherently evil things, they're simply insufficient answers to our questions of security, significance and security.

When we strive, we allow our work to determine our worth, rather than our God-given worth to drive our work. When we strive, we eventually come up short.

4. What feelings or habits have you been unable to overcome or change by sheer will power? How does it feel to know the great apostle Paul faced a similar dilemma?

When we constantly strive, we paint God as a *taskmaster* endlessly demanding that we do it again, do it better, and do more.

When this unsustainable kind of striving leaves us exhausted, overwhelmed, and feeling like it'll never be enough, we hide. Hiding also takes many forms. We can withdraw from relationships or circumstances by mindlessly scrolling through social media, entertain endless *if onlys*, binge on Netflix, start or buy something new, or procrastinate. We can hide behind the temporary satisfaction of food, drink, or other substances.

When we hide, we paint God as *an accuser* who wags His finger, constantly uttering, "Shame on you."

Striving and hiding both promise peace, satisfaction and security, but neither can actually silence the fear that presses on our hearts. No matter how far we run or how well we hide, we cannot escape it. Eventually, both paths (striving and hiding), led to the same pit wallpapered with disappointment, anxiety, more fear, defeat, disconnectedness, loneliness, guilt, restlessness, shame, and discontentment.

5. Reflect on your past week. Is there any evidence of striving or hiding—trying to prove you are enough or being convinced you will never be?

What are we striving for and hiding from? The fear we are not enough—not secure, significant or sufficient enough. **The striver attempts to prove that they are. The hider is convinced that they aren't. Both forget that Jesus already is.** Striving and hiding are both fuelled by lies.

God is not a taskmaster or an accuser, but holy, compassionate, patient, faithful, and loving. He is our all-sufficient heavenly Father who whispers quietly to our hearts an invitation made possible only by the life, death, and resurrection of Jesus Christ: "Come to Me."

6. What do you think God is like? What has led you to that belief? (parents, authority, circumstances, etc.)

    a. Is it true? How do you know?

    b. Are you willing to let God's Word have the final say on what God is like, rather than your experiences? What is actually true of God's character?

    c. How might your perception of what God is like change how willing you are to surrender to Him?

The beautiful alternative to a life of striving and hiding is **surrender.** It's the simple acknowledgement that we are fully known, and in Christ, we are fully loved. He offers Himself to us as a free gift in the great exchange—His righteousness for our filthy rags—all because of His love. The moment you choose to entrust your life to Jesus, by grace through faith, He gives you His.

The next time you feel fear trying to either step on the gas pedal of striving or slam on the brakes of hiding, remember this simple anthem of surrender: **In Christ, I have nothing to prove and nothing to hide.**

Talk to God about it:

He: What has God revealed to you about Himself? Praise, thank or tell Him in the space below.

Me: What has He revealed to you about yourself? What do you need Him to give you, forgive you for or deliver you from? Tell Him in the space below.

We: What do you want Him to do in and through your life by the power of His Spirit? Ask Him here.

Day 3: Hands in the Air

Read it:

12 For the word of God is living and effective and sharper than any double-edged
sword, penetrating as far as the separation of soul and spirit, joints and marrow. It is able to judge
the thoughts and intentions of the heart. 13 No creature is hidden from him, but all things are
naked and exposed to the eyes of him to whom we must give an account. 14 Therefore, since we
have a great high priest who has passed through the heavens—Jesus the Son of God—let us
hold fast to our confession. 15 For we do not have a high priest who is unable to sympathize with
our weaknesses, but one who has been tempted in every way as we are, yet without
sin. 16 Therefore, let us approach the throne of grace with boldness, so that we may receive mercy
and find grace to help us in time of need (Heb. 4:12–16).

Unpack it:

- Underline what the Word is able to do within our hearts (Heb. 4:12).
- Put brackets around the words that describe how we look before the eyes of God (Heb. 4:13).
- Circle the words that describe what kind of high priest Jesus is (Heb. 4:15).
- What is our response to be and what can we expect to find there? (Heb. 4:16).

Work it out:

Do you love God more than you did yesterday? This question posed to me in college always bothered me because at the time, my answer was no. JD Greear says, "In Christ, there's nothing we can do to make God love us more and nothing we have done that can make him love us less."

But can we love God more?

I loved my husband as much as I knew I could the day we said "I do." But after being his wife for over a decade, some things have changed. I'm more aware of the selfishness in me, the sin I'm easily entangled in and the fear I act out of. And when I see how he has loved and continues to love me in light and in spite of myself, I cannot help but love him more.

In the same way, God's love doesn't seem so radical when we think of ourselves as lovely. But as we live a lifestyle of surrender, we begin to see God's unchanging love toward us in our not-so-lovely moments. Love deepens in the soil of gratitude because it makes more room for us to receive.

7. With nothing covering you, how "lovely" do you feel to God? Is it based more on your own loveliness or you being wrapped up in Christ's?

   a. How has God changed your understanding of your own loveliness as you've walked with Him? How has this influenced your gratitude and love towards God?

Hearts that have been packed down by patterns can be softened by surrender.

A lifestyle of surrender requires our humility and faith in His character and compassion. It's allowing God to reveal to us the depth of our sinfulness—which might be a shock to us, but never to Him—and with everything laid bare, choosing to believe Jesus. Uncovered, we keep believing Him. Jesus determined your security, significance and sufficiency on the cross.

He knew what He was getting when He chose you, and He's not changing His mind.

For me, uncovered means admitting that I will never reach the elusive mountaintop of "enough" with only my foothold on the loose gravel of my own strength.

Nothing about me was ever hidden from God's sight even when it was hidden from mine. We don't need to fear being uncovered; we simply need to acknowledge that before God, we already are.

We can live uncovered before God because we are clothed by Christ.[3]

8. One day, we will all be uncovered and laid bare before God to give an account for our lives. How do you feel about that?

[3] Galatians 3:27, Hebrews 4.13.

a. Would you rather God reveal your heart to you today when you can still turn to Jesus to completely cover you, or on that day?

God, who proved[4] His love for us by sending Jesus while we were dead in the water,[5] doesn't need our attempts to prove we are worthy. We can simply believe that Christ's outstretched arms said we are. We can be honest about what we're afraid of, what we don't want to face and how we've been trying to make it go away. We can tell Him that we feel unworthy even if we don't know why.

And in that moment of being broken and bare, we ask Him to plant His truth in the wide-open soil of our hearts where His truth can take root and bear fruit.

I love God more now than I once did, but not because He or His love for me has changed. He is the same yesterday, today and forever. What changed is the frequency and duration of my attempts to strive and hide.

The moments of empty-handed surrender are where I begin to experience the gift and goodness of the gospel. My head has known it, and my heart keeps learning to trust it.

The more I surrender by acknowledging my own depravity and need, contrasted with the backdrop of God's holiness and grace, the greater my experience of the gospel becomes. Grace isn't just the door I came through, it's the reason I can get back up and keep running despite this very imperfect track record. It's not about what I do, but about continuing to believe in what Jesus has done.

9. In Matthew 11:28–30, Jesus declared that rest isn't something we can find on our own, but something we receive when we bring Him our burdens. What does surrender offer that striving and hiding do not?

It is only because of faith in what He has done that we have nothing to prove and nothing to hide. We get to live surrendered. And in this surrender is true rest that only comes from trust.

[4] Romans 5:8.
[5] Ephesians 2:1.

10. How is "life to the full"[6] the same or different from what you are currently experiencing? What would it look like to come to God empty-handed to receive life, rather than trying to achieve it?

Living life to the full requires being filled. To be filled, we need to be empty. And before we can be emptied, our hardened hearts need to be broken open by surrender.

Talk to God about it:

He: What has God revealed to you about Himself? Praise, thank or tell Him in the space below.

Me: What has He revealed to you about yourself? What do you need Him to give you, forgive you for or deliver you from? Tell Him in the space below.

We: What do you want Him to do in and through your life by the power of His Spirit? Ask Him here.

[6] John 10:10.

Day 4: Behind Our Walls

Read it:

17 The righteous cry out, and the Lord hears, and rescues them from all their troubles.
18 The Lord is near the brokenhearted; he saves those crushed in spirit. 19 One who is righteous
has many adversities, but the Lord rescues him from them all (Ps. 34:17–19).

3 He heals the brokenhearted and bandages their wounds (Ps. 147:3).

Unpack it:

- Circle the results when the righteous cry out.
- Underline the five promises the Lord offers to the brokenhearted in the above verses.

Work it out:

When my kids are hurt, they instinctively cover the wounded area. When I try to see and treat the injury, I'm often met with resistance and crying. **It takes a measure of trust for them to believe there is healing past the pain of feeling.**

When we are hurt, we have the same instinct to cover up our pain. We don't like the fact that healing takes time. Instant relief is much preferred. Open wounds feel vulnerable, so we erect walls when something or someone gets too close. Our walls go up with the intent to keep our wounds from hurting more. So, when things get too personal, we pull back. If it's too real, we retreat. And when something stirs in us, we avoid it until the discomfort settles.

11. In what situations do you find yourself feeling defensive or withdrawn? What wounds might be behind your walls?

The soil of our hearts can be hardened by protective walls. The problem with walls is they aren't selective. As long as we don't feel, we assume we're fine. But as our hearts harden, so does our ability to feel on both sides of the emotional spectrum.

In her book, *From Faking It to Finding Grace*, my friend Connie writes: "We don't know how to interpret pain… we process it to mean that perhaps if God would allow this, He must not be trustworthy."[7]

If the rampant presence of evil, pain and suffering in this life doesn't cause you to stop believing in a loving God, it may tempt you to stop trusting Him. After all, how can we trust a God who allows us to experience deep pain?

12. What painful experiences has your life held? What have they influenced you to believe about God? For example, *if God would allow…. then He must be….*

Imagine my surprise when a friend said to me, "I loved being in labour." I've heard people say they loved being pregnant, or love being a mom, but never ever have I heard a person say they loved the excruciating pain of labour. She must have noticed my jaw on the floor because she shrugged and said, "I don't know… when you know there is new life on the other side of all that pain, and you know it's for a reason, you know it's worth it."

This everyday life—the one with all kinds of pain, brokenness and disappointment, is the birth canal to another life.[8] The moment we entrust our lives to Jesus and are spiritually born again, He plants a seed of new life within us. We're going home to heaven where there will be no more pain, fears or tears. **But don't confuse this life with the next. We have glimpses of glory, but in this life, we labour.** On the painful road home marked with suffering, we are called to cling to faith that will take us right through.

Watching my superman of a dad, who never got sick or hurt, physically waste away with ALS was one of the most painful seasons of my life. **I intuitively knew that choosing not to trust God would not change what I was going through, but it would change how I went through it.**

How do we prevent our hearts from hardening in the midst of pain? **Choosing to trust Jesus enough to come to Him instead of covering.** We cannot experience the presence of a sympathetic Saviour who weeps with us in our pain,[9] is deeply grieved and sorrowful over the death sin causes, and who is sympathetic in every way without coming to Him.

Let pain prompt us to fix our eyes on Jesus, the One who knows pain because He paid for all of it. Every lack can be an invitation to look to Him with our tear-filled eyes. Instead of a lecture to

[7] Connie Cavanaugh, *From Faking It to Finding Grace: Discovering God Again When Your Faith Runs Dry* (Eugene, OR: Harvest House Publishers, 2005).
[8] Romans 8:18–25.
[9] John 11:35.

stop crying because one day it'll all be okay, perhaps we'll be met with the kind, sympathetic, tear-filled eyes that understand life was not meant to be this way.[10]

Let pain remind you that this world is not our home. The reason it feels like it's not supposed to be this way is because it wasn't.

13. Does believing you have a sympathetic Saviour, who weeps with you and has all the mercy and grace you need, change your willingness to come to Him in your weakness? What do you expect to be met with?

We can offer praise from the pit of pain, trusting His character when His actions feel confusing. He never wastes our pain but promises eternal glory that is not worth comparing to our present suffering.[11]

Invite the Truth Himself into your pain. He wants to heal and waits for you to ask. **We are free to feel when we trust Him to heal.**

[10] John 11:32–28.
[11] Romans 8:18, 2 Corinthians 4:16–18.

Talk to God about it:

He: What has God revealed to you about Himself? Praise, thank or tell Him in the space below.

Me: What has He revealed to you about yourself? What do you need Him to give you, forgive you for or deliver you from? Tell Him in the space below.

We: What do you want Him to do in and through your life by the power of His Spirit? Ask Him here.

Day 5: Before the Fall

Read it:

4 In his pride the wicked man does not seek him; in all his thoughts there is no room for God (Ps. 10:4).

12 Before his downfall a person's heart is proud, but humility comes before honour (Prov. 18:12).

23 This is what the Lord says: "The wise person should not boast in his wisdom; the strong should not boast in his strength; the wealthy should not boast in his wealth. 24 But the one who boasts should boast in this: that he understands and knows me—that I am the Lord, showing faithful love, justice, and righteousness on the earth, for I delight in these things. This is the Lord's declaration" (Jer. 9:23–24).

17 "Let the one who boasts, boast in the Lord." 18 For it is not the one who commends himself who is approved, but the one whom the Lord commends (2 Cor. 10:17–18).

Unpack it:

- Circle the four words that describe the evidence of not seeking God due to pride (Ps. 10:4).
- Underline the result of a prideful heart, and what precedes honour (Prov. 18:12).
- Put brackets around what we are to boast in (Jer. 9:24).
- What are we to boast in and why? (2 Cor. 10:17–18).

Work it out:

"You always have to have it your way," my classmate pointed out. **I was fired up because I felt found out.** My teenaged self was selfishly thinking, "It's because my way is better." It wasn't the first time I wanted things done my way—I came out of the womb bossy—and it certainly wasn't the first or last time I was convinced my way was best. When my way was best, I felt valuable. When my way was *the* way, it gave me the sense of significance my heart was desperately searching for.

Pride is defined in the Oxford Dictionary as *a feeling or deep pleasure or satisfaction derived from one's own achievements, the achievements of those with whom one is closely associated, or from qualities or possessions that are widely admired.*

Pride wears many hats. It can masquerade as self-sufficiency and independence, both highly praised and prized qualities in our culture. It can look like stubbornness or an unwillingness to admit when we're in the wrong. Pride is poison because as the psalmist says, it leaves no room for God. We might not shout it from the rooftops, but we quietly allow our own beliefs, ideas, ways, desires, plans, opinions or feelings *to lead* instead of follow.

In addition to our patterns and protective walls, our hearts can become packed down by pride, and as a result, truth cannot take root. An unwillingness to let go, change, or surrender may signal an area hardened with pride.

If the contents of your heart were laid bare before God, what would you cling to with clenched fists? Your achievements? Your emotional reactions? Your tightly packed or neatly planned schedule? Your excuses? Your parenting style? The company you keep? Your drug of choice?

14. What are you tempted to hold onto tightly? What makes you feel reluctant about letting go?

Jesus has already staked the claim to having all the trump cards when it comes to whose way is best. He said, **"I am the way, the truth and the life. No one comes to the Father except through me."**[12]

To let go of our pride and make the soil of our hearts available to Him, we must surrender our hearts, minds, and wills to Him completely. Humility is the only road out of a heart hardened by pride and it can begin with a prayer as simple as **"Thine, not mine."** Our wandering hearts need the continual reminder that following Jesus is just that—following. He leads, we follow.

King David wrote this prayer: "Search me, O God, and know my heart… See if there is any offensive way in me, and lead me in the way everlasting."[13]

By aligning our ways with His, we take on the posture opposite to pride—humility.

Confidence in Christ allows us to have an attitude of humility because we no longer need to prove ourselves worthy by being right.

15. Does believing you are wholly loved, accepted and secured by Christ's righteousness enable you to release your desire to be in charge to Him? If not, what keeps you from letting go?

[12] John 14:6.
[13] Psalm 139:23–24.

God began to chip away at my pride as I realized that "being right" was not what He required of me. Instead, He required righteousness. Right standing with Him came only by placing my life in His. Jesus has secured me with His righteousness. I'm free to do what is right, rather than having a white-knuckled grip on always being right. When I let go of my own way, my hands are free to submit to His. And His way is always the way to life.

16. Why might boasting in the Lord be wiser than boasting in ourselves? Who has the final say over us—our gifts, our worth and our lives?

Talk to God about it:

He: What has God revealed to you about Himself? Praise, thank or tell Him in the space below.

Me: What has He revealed to you about yourself? What do you need Him to give you, forgive you for or deliver you from? Tell Him in the space below.

We: What do you want Him to do in and through your life by the power of His Spirit? Ask Him here.

Day 6: The Peril of the Path

Read it:

[17] The sacrifice pleasing to God is a broken spirit. You will not despise a broken and humbled heart, God (Ps. 51:17).

[10] My goal is to know him and the power of his resurrection and the fellowship of his sufferings, being conformed to his death (Phil. 3:10).

Unpack it:

- Circle the kind of sacrifice that is pleasing to God (Ps. 51:17).
- Underline the two descriptors of what God will not despise (Ps. 51:17).
- Circle the two words that describe Paul's goal (Phil. 3:10).
- Underline two other things involved with knowing Christ besides the power of the resurrection (Phil. 3:10).

Work it out:

We live under the pressure to "have it all together," and sometimes we may even think it's within our reach. This illusion takes just moments to be shattered. For me, that happened with a single phone call on May 5, 2008.

My dad called to tell me the neurologist had given him bad news. He had ALS, it was fatal, and at the time, they thought he had three to five years to live.

My dad's illness revealed brokenness in the world and in my own heart that my patterns, protectiveness and pride could not fix. **No amount of striving would change the prognosis, and no amount of hiding would make it go away.**

Though we are all uncomfortable with feeling helpless, the most difficult seasons can be the most fertile soil if we are willing to meet Jesus in our weakness.

Ultimately, unwillingness to admit brokenness makes our hearts impenetrable, and patterns, protectiveness and pride continue to harden our hearts. It's not that Truth cannot break in, but He often waits for an invitation. Even the tiniest bit of surrender, trust or humility is enough of an indication that there is an invitation.

17. How comfortable are you with acknowledging brokenness in your life? Did your family of origin allow room for imperfection or weakness? Was weakness viewed negatively or positively, as the beginning point of strength?

Unfortunately, we don't have to feel convicted about our patterns, protectiveness or pride to experience the consequences of them. Unwillingness to acknowledge our brokenness only further blinds our eyes, deafens our ears and hardens our hearts. To even begin recognizing our brokenness, we must ask the only One who can make our eyes see, our ears hear, and our hearts understand.[14] Will you trust God enough to ask?

18. Have you experienced (or seen someone else experience) God's strength in the midst of brokenness? Describe the difference He made below.

God is not an unrelenting taskmaster with a sledgehammer, threatening us to come out or else, and nor is he an accuser looking to publicly humiliate us by revealing our guilt and shame. He is patient, full of loving-kindness and compassion. He invites us to humbly ask Him to break through our hardened hearts in a way that only He can so that we can experience His life in us. And, so others will see Him in us, and experience life as well.

But what if we don't?

The peril of the path is this: where there is no brokenness, there is no openness.

Brokenness is what we need. It is the only way a hardened heart opens. This cannot be accomplished by force, but by realizing that we are too weak to do it ourselves. When the striver in you shouts "work harder," or your inner hider whispers, "you'll never change," remember Jesus paved the way to the Father. The work is finished.

Because of Jesus, death is not the end but the beginning. On the other side of death is His resurrection power. The word resurrection (anastasis) means: *standing on the feet again or rising as opposed to falling; to rise again from the spiritual death of sin.*[15] Scripture tells us the same power that raised Jesus from the dead lives inside of us, but we can't access it without death.

[14] Matthew 13:13–15.

[15] *Strong's*, G386, "anastasis," G386, https://www.blueletterbible.org/lang/lexicon/lexicon.cfm?Strongs=G386&t=NIV.

Jesus didn't come so the good could be better; He came so the dead could be alive. In clinging to our patterns, protectiveness and pride, we stand in the way of His work. Sometimes we don't want to die to our sin until we get a glimpse of the suffering our sin brings with it. We don't need new sin; we simply need new eyes to see the suffering our sin has caused. Perhaps these glimpses would make us more willing to die.

19. What has sin cost you and those you love? What kind of suffering has it brought with it?

We cannot rise again in the power of Christ if we have not died to ourselves.

We have to be utterly convinced our patterns, protectiveness and pride will not deliver what it is that we truly want. If you don't want to die to yourself, ask God to show you what your hardness of heart is killing or keeping you from. He will not transform the path into good soil without brokenness.

20. What is keeping you from wanting to die to your patterns, protectiveness and pride?

We can surrender our weakness without offering solutions to accompany it. Surrender has no prerequisites. The Healer doesn't require our hearts to come whole; He takes them weak, broken and bare.

Our weakness is where we experience Jesus' completeness.

Are you willing to trust Jesus with your weakness?

It is not a barrier to the flourishing life, it is the way to it. What we do with our weakness will determine whether or not we flourish. Everywhere there is brokenness, there is openness for seeds of transformation to be planted.

Talk to God about it:

He: What has God revealed to you about Himself? Praise, thank or tell Him in the space below.

Me: What has He revealed to you about yourself? What do you need Him to give you, forgive you for or deliver you from? Tell Him in the space below.

We: What do you want Him to do in and through your life by the power of His Spirit? Ask Him here.

Day 7: Reflect

Look Back at the Path:

When you look over the last six days of responses, do you see a theme emerging? Ask the Holy Spirit to highlight what He wants you to remember.

- What patterns is God asking you to exchange for surrender?

- What protective walls is He asking you to exchange for trusting Him?

- How does He want you to trade your pride for humility?

Summarize what God has been teaching you in 2 to 3 sentences.

If you are willing, write out a prayer of surrender in response to what God reveals:

Video session 2 is available at http://everydaytruth.ca/flourish

Session 2: Softened by Surrender

James 1:19–21

1. Be quick to ________________.
    - Becoming a quick listener means continually trading ______________________ for ______________________ before ______________________

2. Slow down your ____________________.

3. Slow down your ____________________.
    - ANGER: movement or __________________ of the soul; __________________, ______________, or any violent emotion;
    - Slowing down our impulses is what ________ us to __________ what might be beneath them.
    - STRIVING is any attempt to ______________________ feeling secure, sufficient or significant.
    - HIDING is any attempt to ________________ feeling insecure, insufficient or insignificant

QUICK, SLOW, SLOW, makes room to ___________________________

SAVE: to save, keep safe and sound, to rescue from danger or destruction; to save a suffering one from perishing, i.e. One suffering from disease, to __________ ______________, ______________, restore to health; to preserve one who is in danger of destruction, to save or ______________.

Weakness cannot _______________ the good news; it is the intersection to ___________________ it.

What we do with weakness will determine whether or not we ________________________.

Session 2 Reflection/Discussion Questions:

1. What has God been teaching you about the condition of your heart as you've studied this week?

2. Do you tend to react or ask before acting? What consequences of either have you experienced?

3. What attempts at striving or hiding have you seen in your own life?

4. How have you interpreted weakness up until this point in your life? Have you seen it as an intersection to experience Jesus? How might that perspective shift how you interpret weakness in your own life and the lives of those around you?

5. What do you sense God is teaching you right now?

The Rocks

Day 8: The Rocky Reality

Read it:

[20] And the one sown on rocky ground—this is one who hears the word and immediately receives it with joy. [21] But he has no root and is short-lived. When distress or persecution comes because of the word, immediately he falls away (Matt. 13:20–21).

[2] Every branch in me that does not produce fruit he removes, and he prunes every branch that produces fruit so that it will produce more fruit (John 15:2).

Unpack it:

- Put brackets around the way the hearer on the rocky ground receives the word (Matt. 13:20).
- Underline the reality of the plant in rocky soil and the result (Matt. 13:21a).
- Circle the two things that cause falling away (Matt. 13:21b).
- What is the destiny of a fruitless branch? (John 15:2).

Work it out:

As a teenager, I attended an annual youth conference and summer camp with my youth group. Spending time with masses of like-minded people submerged in worship and the Word was a shot of spiritual adrenaline. I remember both fondly.

After a few years, a pattern emerged. Within a couple of weeks of returning home, many would report their enthusiasm had dwindled. The countdown to the next high would begin.

We don't automatically grow out of this pattern. As adults, the next spiritual high can be the conference, the retreat, or the Sunday worship service.

Don't get me wrong, I love gathering with the body of Christ. My ministry involves gathering with women around the Word. When you bring hundreds of candles together, you get a bonfire. There is a special presence of the Holy Spirit when the body of Christ gathers.

Conferences, retreats, services and studies leave us feeling spiritually high. But within days or weeks, the enthusiasm and resolve from the spark of spiritual adrenaline fades. Time and time again, we discover this sobering truth in our spiritual lives:

Sparks can start fires, but they cannot sustain them.

21. Think back to a time when you felt spiritually "sparked." Was it sustained, or did you soon find yourself stumbling? What were the contributing factors?

A seed sown in a rocky heart is characterized by enthusiasm without endurance. A seed with no room to develop deep-roots yields a crop that withers easily under the elements.

Endurance requires sustenance. How is a fire sustained? By continually giving it fuel. Without it, a fire will inevitably fade.

22. When you think of the word, "endurance," what comes to mind? What characterized a season where you endured with something or someone? What was the result?

While the harvest of the path yields nothing at all, the rocky ground makes for an equally anticlimactic harvest. The initial excitement of springing up can temporarily distract from the fact that a withered crop is as useless to the farmer as no crop at all.

23. Have you ever been enthusiastic about a spiritual truth but distracted from being transformed by it? Describe it below.

Over the next few days, we will wrestle with this question: **how do we establish strong spiritual roots so that we stand firm rather than stumble when faced with pressure and persecution?**

Talk to God about it:

He: What has God revealed to you about Himself? Praise, thank or tell Him in the space below.

Me: What has He revealed to you about yourself? What do you need Him to give you, forgive you for or deliver you from? Tell Him in the space below.

We: What do you want Him to do in and through your life by the power of His Spirit? Ask Him here.

Day 9: Hardscaping

Read it:

[5] Other seed fell on rocky ground where it didn't have much soil, and it grew up quickly since the soil wasn't deep. [6] But when the sun came up, it was scorched, and since it had no root, it withered away (Matt. 13:5–6).

Unpack it:

- Underline the words that describe the rocky ground (Matt. 13:5).
- Circle the result of having no root in the scorching heat of the sun (Matt. 13:6).

Work it out:

Outdoor living landscapes, as I have learned from my avid HGTV watching, are made up of two components: hardscapes and softscapes. Hardscapes describe the inanimate features such as walkways, retaining walls, pavers, and other structures, whereas softscapes include living elements such as flowers, grass, trees, shrubs and groundcovers. When properly combined, they make beautiful and functional outdoor living spaces.

If the goal is only to be beautiful and functional, hardscaping will deliver. But if the goal is productivity of the soil, it won't. **Rocks are not alive and therefore cannot, and do not, enhance the soil's productivity.**

Our own ways are like rocks. They might appear beautiful and functional but they do not have the ability within themselves to produce life. **Our ways can get in the way of The Way.**

24. What in your life has been like "hardscapes"—functional but not productive for the kingdom?

What Jesus describes as the rocky ground means *underlying shallow soil or a ground full of rocks.*[16] When soil has underlying rock, it lacks depth. Roots cannot be established when rocks occupy valuable real estate in our hearts.

[16] Strong's, G4075, "petrodes," https://www.blueletterbible.org/lang/lexicon/lexicon.cfm?Strongs=G4075&t=NASB.

The rocks in our hearts eventually cause stumbling. To stumble means *to put a stumbling block or impediment in the way upon which another may trip and fall; to entice to sin; to cause a person to begin to distrust and desert one whom he ought to trust and obey; to cause to fall away.*[17]

Did you catch that? The heart filled with rocks eventually begins *to distrust and desert one whom he ought to trust and obey.* **While the path is characterized by unwillingness to trust God with our weakness, the rocky ground is characterized by unwillingness to trust God with our ways.**

Our "rocks," or our ways can be difficult to detect because they are highly praised and prized in our world. If we're not careful, we camouflage right into culture, not realizing that we're living contrary to God's ways. Here are a few "rocks" I've seen surface in my own life:

The world says be self-sufficient; *the Word says to be dependent on the Spirit.*
The world says earn it; *the Word says it's given to you.*
The world says to achieve; *the Word says to receive.*
The world says stay busy and hustle; *the Word says to Sabbath as a sign of trust.*
The world says it's never enough; *the Word says celebrate and rejoice.*
The world says you need more; *the Word says to be content with what you have.*
The world says you don't need people; *the Word says you were made for community.*
The world says stay in control; *the Word says Someone already is.*

Without openly objecting to God's ways, we can still live in quiet rebellion by doing things our own way. Thankfully, our ways are not too difficult for the Holy Spirit to discern when we ask Him to search our hearts.

25. Which of your ways might be most difficult to surrender to God? Your pace? Time? Schedule? Reactions? Margin? Tone of voice? Priorities? How might surrendering a "rock" make room to become rooted in Him?

Our ways seem like a means to an end to get what we want, but like rocks, they cannot bring life. They may even help us function, but in the end, they do not make us alive. **To retrieve the nutrients needed to survive, roots need room.**

Ask God to make some room in your heart for His ways.

[17] *Strong's*, G4624, "skandalizo," https://www.blueletterbible.org/lang/lexicon/lexicon.cfm?Strongs=G4624&t=NASB.

Talk to God about it:

He: What has God revealed to you about Himself? Praise, thank or tell Him in the space below.

Me: What has He revealed to you about yourself? What do you need Him to give you, forgive you for or deliver you from? Tell Him in the space below.

We: What do you want Him to do in and through your life by the power of His Spirit? Ask Him here.

Day 10: Which Way?

Read it:

[12] There is a way that seems right to a person, but its end is the way to death (Prov. 14:12).

[18] There is one who speaks rashly, like a piercing sword; but the tongue of the wise brings healing (Prov. 12:18).

Unpack it:

- Circle the words that describe a person's perception of their own way (Prov. 14:12).
- Underline what it is the way to (Prov. 14:12).
- Put brackets around the words that describe a person who speaks rashly (Prov. 12:18).
- Circle the word that describes what the tongue of the wise brings (Prov. 12:18).

Work it out:

When the weather permits, we do school drop-off on our bikes. There are a few possible routes—roads, bike paths, and grassy shortcuts we can take that all get us to school. We choose based on which way will get us what we think we want. On some mornings we want efficiency, while on others we want the path of least resistance.

We tend to make life choices in the same manner—what seems like the good, better and best way? But perhaps we can ask a wiser question: **Is this the way to life?** While a variety of routes will eventually lead us to school, there are not a variety of ways that lead to life.

When we approach God's way as just one of many options, we fool ourselves into thinking all roads lead to the same place. They don't. Jesus laid exclusive claim to being the way, the truth and the life.[18] **We will not find the narrow way to life or to flourishing apart from living His way.**

26. Do you act/think as though Jesus' way is a better way or the only way? How so?

[18] John 14:6

While I have trusted and obeyed some of God's ways without much resistance, I have silently rebelled at others by delaying obedience. My own personal caveats for obedience have resulted in costly consequences—a degree of death.

As a newlywed wife, I was trying to decode my husband's new role—spiritual head.[19] Neither of us knew exactly what it looked like. I grew up seeing my dad (who was also my pastor) engaging in many regular spiritual disciplines. In my mind, a spiritually disciplined man was deserving of respect.

It didn't occur to me that God commanding my respect for my husband had more to do with His design for life than with my idea of deserving.

Respect was a necessary ingredient to my husband becoming the man God intended, but I was too busy acting as judge to offer it. Not only did I not have a clue what respect looked and sounded like, but I silently exempted myself because he wasn't up to his eyeballs in spiritual disciplines.

I'm ashamed to say it, but my thought process was, "If you do what is respectable in my opinion, then I'll respect you." Just imagine how horrified I would've felt if he had lived by the same standard, "I'll love you only when you're lovable in my opinion."

I was doing it my way and it was rocky. But the even bigger problem was that it was a dead way. Withholding what my husband needed didn't inspire him to change; it made it impossible.

The fruit of doing things my way was death.[20] I killed the emotional safety in our marriage with my nagging. A flawed human trying to play the Holy Spirit made following God unappealing. And I helped make sin seem more enticing. Twice, we are warned in Proverbs of the ways that seem right to us but its end is the way to death.[21]

27. What has been the fruit of trying to find life apart from God's ways? In your heart? In your relationships? In your spiritual life?

As God began to change my ways, infusing respect into the way I communicated, guess what happened? Slowly but surely, I watched my husband come more alive in Christ. My obedience to God's way breathed life into my marriage, not because of me, but because God's way is life.

[19] Ephesians 5:23.
[20] Romans 6:21–23.
[21] Proverbs 14:12, Proverbs 16:25.

Delayed obedience is really just disobedience.

Disobedience to the truth is sin. Sin always leads to death, no matter why we did it in the first place.

What relationship, circumstance or person in your life might be experiencing death because of your way? Confess your way to God. It'll make more room for His.

Talk to God about it:

He: What has God revealed to you about Himself? Praise, thank or tell Him in the space below.

Me: What has He revealed to you about yourself? What do you need Him to give you, forgive you for or deliver you from? Tell Him in the space below.

We: What do you want Him to do in and through your life by the power of His Spirit? Ask Him here.

Day 11: The High Way?

Read it:

21 But he has no root and is short-lived. When distress or persecution comes because of the word, immediately he falls away (Matt. 16:21).

21 When a woman is giving birth, she has sorrow because her hour has come, but when she has delivered the baby, she no longer remembers the anguish, for joy that a human being has been born into the world (John 16:21).

16 I pray that he may grant you, according to the riches of his glory, to be strengthened with power in your inner being through his Spirit, 17 and that Christ may dwell in your hearts through faith. I pray that you, being rooted and firmly established in love, 18 may be able to comprehend with all the saints what is the length and width, height and depth of God's love, 19 and to know Christ's love that surpasses knowledge, so that you may be filled with all the fullness of God (Eph. 3:14–20).

16 Rejoice always, 17 pray constantly, 18 give thanks in everything; for this is God's will for you in Christ Jesus (1 Thess. 5:16–18).

Unpack it:

- Circle the first of the two circumstances that cause a rocky heart to fall away (Matt. 13:21).
- Underline the scenario that helps us understand the "anguish" John writes about (John 16:21).
- Put brackets around each of the things Paul prays for the believers (Eph. 3:16–20).
- Underline the big three instructions described as "God's will for you in Christ" (1 Thess. 5:16–18).

Work it out:

When I was nearing my due date with baby #3, I was in no hurry to deliver. I was excited to meet our little one, but I knew full well what stood between me and that moment—labour. When it began, my amnesia was shattered and vivid memories of the pain that lay ahead resurfaced. My immediate thought was, "I don't want to do this!"

But not wanting to endure it didn't exempt me from the fact that the only way out was through.

In John 16:21, Jesus describes how a woman forgets the anguish of labour because of the joy the new life staring back at her brings. The word "anguish" here is the same word that is translated "distress" in the Parable of the Sower. Distress or pressure causes stumbling for a growing seed surrounded by rocks rather than room to put down strong roots. **In labour, pressure makes us push through, but in life, pressure can make us pull back.**

28. How has being under pressure either caused you to push through and/or pull back from walking in God's ways?

Have you faced enough pressure to realize deep roots and rocks can't thrive together? **We cannot be deeply rooted in rocky soil.** Paul prayed that we would be strengthened on the inside so that we could be rooted and grounded in the love of Christ.[22] How do our roots get grounded in the love of Christ?

We can do what Scripture says is His will.[23] In everything—the unknown, the waiting, the present difficulties—we can choose to be joyful, prayerful and thankful. Obedience is life even when we don't feel like it. When we don't obey, the rocks of joylessness, prayerlessness and thanklessness fill the soil of our hearts and stay in the way of our own roots.

29. When is it the most difficult for you to be joyful? What is the fruit of joylessness?

30. When is it the most difficult for you to be prayerful? What is the fruit of prayerlessness?

[22] Ephesians 3:14–20.
[23] 1 Thessalonians 5:16–18.

31. When is it the most difficult for you to be thankful? What is the fruit of thanklessness?

32. What might the fruit of a joyful, prayerful and thankful life be?

We must be willing to actually obey His ways, continually surrendering our own. Jesus described the one who heard His words and put them into practice as a wise man who built his house on a rock and a foolish man who did not put His words into practice as a foolish man who built his house on the sand.[24]

33. What are some of your own ways you've clung to, knowing they're not God's? How has that affected your spiritual root system?

As we trust Jesus is the Way and He is Life, our roots have room to reach deep to find what we need in Him.

[24] Matthew 7:24–27.

Talk to God about it:

He: What has God revealed to you about Himself? Praise, thank or tell Him in the space below.

Me: What has He revealed to you about yourself? What do you need Him to give you, forgive you for or deliver you from? Tell Him in the space below.

We: What do you want Him to do in and through your life by the power of His Spirit? Ask Him here.

Day 12: How Deep Is Your Love?

Read it:

[5] Other seed fell on rocky ground where it didn't have much soil, and it grew up quickly, since the soil wasn't deep. [6] When the sun came up, it was scorched, and since it had no root, it withered away (Mark 4:5–6).

[38] The one who believes in me, as the Scripture has said, will have streams of living water flow from deep within him" (John 7:38).

[13] For my people have committed a double evil: They have abandoned me, the fountain of living water, and dug cisterns for themselves—cracked cisterns that cannot hold water (Jer. 2:13).

Unpack it:

- Circle the result of no root (Mark 4:5).
- Underline the result of believing in Jesus (John 7:38).
- Put brackets around what God's people abandoned and circle what they got in exchange (Jer. 2:13).

Work it out:

When we moved into our current home, a friend gave me a daylily as a housewarming gift. At that point, the only plant that had survived under my care was made of silk. Though I lacked confidence in my gardening skills, I was assured the daylily was hardy and forgiving. Sure enough, my nearly-withered plant was revived numerous times by simply watering it.

Withering doesn't happen in an instant. It happens slowly and surely as a plant is deprived of moisture. The way to revive a thirsty, withered plant is to water it.

The way to revive a thirsty, withered heart is to connect it with Living Water.

34. What does withering look like in your life when you aren't connected to Living Water?

Jesus declared that Living Water—a well of water springing up within for eternal life—was available to those who asked Him for it.[25] Later, He added that whoever believed in Him would have streams of water flow from within.[26]

How do our thirsty hearts stay rooted in the love of Jesus and flow with Living Water? We start by confessing that doing things our way isn't an alternative path to life.

Jesus' way is not simply the best way; it is the only way to be truly alive.

The more we practise His ways, the deeper and more established in Him our roots become. To continue in our own ways rather than His is like abandoning the fountain of Living Water for cracked cisterns that cannot hold water.[27] **When we choose the cracked cisterns of our own ways, if we are in Christ we are not condemned,[28] but we are thirsty.**

We also must remember that reviving a withered plant takes time. While waiting, we need to stay connected to Water by continuing to walk His way.

Have you ever noticed that water always travels down? Living Water is found on our knees, not on our toes. Humility is the posture that keeps us ready to turn around the moment we find ourselves going our own way. As He floods the deepest places in our heart, He will overflow.

His will isn't for us to get low once, but to live low. Performance will eventually wither just like an enthusiastic shoot without roots; connection will not. Connection is strengthened by communication from a posture of humility. We must keep asking, seeking and knocking on His door for what we cannot do for ourselves.

We can't grow high without first getting low.

35. How have you tried to "reach" God by growing high (performance), instead of getting low (connection)? Describe the result.

[25] John 4:13–15.
[26] John 7:38.
[27] Jeremiah 2:13.
[28] Romans 8:1.

36. Do you think of humbling yourself as something that happened once when you came to Christ, or is it a habit? Do you tend to get low (humble yourself occasionally), or do you live low (in a continual posture of humility)?

37. How do you feel about "living low" in a posture of continual humility? What adjustments are needed for you to do so?

Without water, a plant is scorched by the heat and light of the sun. But if a plant is deeply rooted in good soil and connected to water, the heat and light of the sun will cause it to grow the roots, then shoots, and eventually, it will bear fruit. Shoots can support fruit if the roots are well established.

We are made for fruit, but not before roots.

Talk to God about it:

He: What has God revealed to you about Himself? Praise, thank or tell Him in the space below.

Me: What has He revealed to you about yourself? What do you need Him to give you, forgive you for or deliver you from? Tell Him in the space below.

We: What do you want Him to do in and through your life by the power of His Spirit? Ask Him here.

Day 13: The Reality of the Rocks

Read it:

[16] For God loved the world in this way: He gave his one and only Son, so that everyone who believes in him will not perish but have eternal life (John 3:16).

[21] The one who has my commands and keeps them is the one who loves me. And the one who loves me will be loved by my Father. I also will love him and will reveal myself to him" (John 14:21).

[6] So then, just as you have received Christ Jesus as Lord, continue to live in him, [7] being rooted and built up in him and established in the faith, just as you were taught, and overflowing with gratitude (Col. 2:6–7).

Unpack it:

- What did God prove by giving Jesus to the world so they would have eternal life? (John 3:16).
- Circle Jesus' description of the one who loves Him (John 14:21).
- What are the three results for the one who loves Jesus?
- Underline the action that is to follow receiving Christ Jesus as Lord (Col. 2:6–7).
- What four things result from continuing to live in Christ?

Work it out:

When I assign a task to my children, I can predict fairly accurately who will obey and who will delay. When I ask them to put on their coats and shoes, I know which child will need wrangling, which one will need constant reminders, and which one will be standing by the door ready to go.

Does this cause me to love one more than the others?

No. My love for them is secured by the fact that they belong to me. Behaviour cannot undo their belonging. Yet the question lingers—what does obedience influence?

Their obedience displays their level of trust in me, which ultimately shows their love for me. When I see that my child trusts me enough to obey without delay, something happens. There is a special echo of love from my heart to their own that they experience as they respond in obedience.

38. How have seasons of obeying or delaying with God influenced your experience of His love for you?

Similarly, there is great rest and deep relief in knowing that God's love for us rests on the life of Jesus, not our own. We can't earn it, deserve it or undo it. God's love for the world was so great that He sent Jesus to save it. It has been secured.

Yet this truth is tucked into John 14:21—"The one who loves me will be loved by my Father." If Jesus has already secured the love of God for us, what love is He talking about here?

It would seem that in a similar way that my love echoes between my obedient child and me, there's some sort of reverberation of God's love unlocked when one's love for Jesus is displayed by obedience to His commands.

In addition to this reverberation of love, there's a readiness that obedience accomplishes in us.

I know who I can rely on to complete the task with the least resistance. My coatless children are not condemned, nor do they cease to belong to me, but they're not prepared for what I have planned. I don't tell them to get ready without reason, nor do I tell them to pack their school lunches simply for the sake of seeing them labour. I know what the weather forecast holds, what the demands of the day will bring, and what they'll need to get through it.

I have a little tune that goes like this: **"Okay, then obey, right away, no delay. Anytime you can ask along the way."**

I know who is ready for more responsibility based on their track record. As we walk in obedience to God's ways, we experience His love and we ready ourselves for His work. Sadly, many believers never emerge from the classroom of obedience ready for the work God has called them to do.

They are no less loved by God, but they are not ready. The spiritual muscle of faith and obedience that the race so often requires has not been built. This is not about condemnation—we have none if we are in Christ. This is about consequences.

We are physical beings that live within a spiritual reality. Sometimes there are no immediately observable physical consequences to our obedience or disobedience. But don't be fooled into thinking this is the same as nothing happening. Scripture tells us that we are to focus not on what is seen, but on what is unseen.[29] Though our spiritual reality (the consequences experienced in our hearts, minds, bodies and souls) is unseen, it is very real.

39. What are some consequences of obedience you've experienced in your life?

    a. What are some consequences of disobedience you've experienced in your life?

Will the love of God reverberate through your life? Will you be ready for the race He has set before you? Can your heavenly Father trust you to carry out His work? Are you willing to build your obedience muscles today?

Start walking in His ways. You need them to be ready for the work He has prepared and planned for you to do, and you'll want His love reverberating through your heart as you do it.

Talk to God about it:

He: What has God revealed to you about Himself? Praise, thank or tell Him in the space below.

Me: What has He revealed to you about yourself? What do you need Him to give you, forgive you for or deliver you from? Tell Him in the space below.

We: What do you want Him to do in and through your life by the power of His Spirit? Ask Him here.

[29] 2 Corinthians 4:18.

Day 14: Reflect

Look Back at the Rocks:

When you look over the last six days of responses, do you see a theme emerging? Ask the Holy Spirit to highlight what He wants you to remember.

- What has God been revealing to you about your way of doing things?
- Which of your ways are you tempted to cling most tightly to?
- What ways do you sense He's asking you to exchange for His own?

Summarize what God has been teaching you in 2 to 3 sentences.

If you are willing, write out a prayer of surrender in response to what God reveals:

Video session 3 is available at http://everydaytruth.ca/flourish

Session 3: The Reveal

Tough times ________________ the rugs that make us prone to ____________________.

1. Choose to ________________________.

2. Choose to ________________________.

3. Choose to ________________________.

Session 3 Reflection/Discussion Questions:

1. We know because of the promise in Romans 8:1 that if we are in Christ, there is no condemnation over our lives. Jesus has declared us not guilty of the death that sin causes. What consequences have you experienced?

2. What do you anticipate will make it difficult to walk in God's ways in the next 24 hours? In the next week? What encouragement will you need from the Holy Spirit and your community? Ask them for it now.

3. Which of God's ways are you committing to this week with the Holy Spirit's help so that your spiritual roots can go down deep into the love of Christ?

4. One problem we of little faith have is we tend to think God's ways are arbitrary and optional. Woven into God's ways exclusively is the flourishing life that you and I so desperately long for.

    a. What might happen in your heart, mind, relationships as you walk in God's ways this week?

    b. What might happen if you don't?

    c. Revisit your answers a week from now and see if the consequences (positive or negative) are what you anticipated they would be.

The Thorns

Day 15: The No-Berry Bush

Read it:

7 Other seed fell among thorns, and the thorns came up and choked it (Matt. 13:7).

22 Now the one sown among the thorns—this is one who hears the word, but the worries of this age and the deceitfulness of wealth choke the word, and it becomes unfruitful (Matt. 13:22).

Unpack it:

- Circle the result of the thorns coming up (Matt. 13:7).
- Underline the two things that choke the Word (Matt. 13:22a).
- Put brackets around the result (Matt. 13:22b).

Work it out:

When we moved into our current home, the landscaping in our backyard wasn't ready to roll, but I was. I was determined to plant fruit bushes even though my garden didn't have the space for them to thrive.

The rebel in me waved my hand and decided it would be fine. I planted a haskap berry bush in a one-by-ten-foot garden box intending to move it to a larger spot well before it grew to its potential five-by-five feet. I should mention that this garden box was also home to four blueberry and two strawberry plants. It may have been a tad crowded.

All seemed well in the first few seasons. The haskap bush was growing like a weed and was extremely fruitful—so much so that my children's summer snack time could be berries picked in the backyard.

After a few years in, all the plants displayed evidence of life and growth, but as the summer wore on, it became evident that the berry bushes were not living up to their name. There was no fruit to enjoy—not a single haskap berry, blueberry or strawberry.

As baby bushes, they were able to grow and produce, but as their root systems attempted to grow in crowded soil, they were unable to access the nutrients needed to bear fruit. **There was too much competition.** It was a disappointing harvest, to say the least.

In the parable of the Sower, the seed sown on the path produced no crop. The seed sown on rocky ground had immediate growth but eventually became a withered crop. The seed sown among thorns was growing, but eventually it was a choked crop. Which of these crops would a farmer be *most* interested in?

It's easy to assume the farmer would be happier with the seed sown in thorny soil but the truth is, no matter how much growth there was, none of the seeds sown produced what they were made to produce: *actual fruit.*

While the disappointment over the seed sown in the thorny soil would be delayed, at the end of the day, the end result would be just as useless as a withered crop.

Don't get me wrong—spiritual growth *is* exciting. We should mark significant spiritual milestones and celebrate growth without forgetting that the goal of our lives isn't only to increase our time spent in the Word or serving, though those will help us grow. If we make growth the goal, it can distract us from the point of being a branch.

A branch doesn't exist only to grow; fruit is to be produced through it.

It cannot produce fruit unless it is connected to the source. Jesus described the seed sown among thorns as one who hears the word, in whom it takes root, maybe even grows shoots, but ultimately bears no fruit.

Thorny soil, much like my crowded garden box, chokes fruit production.

> To choke means *to press around, to throng (a pressing increase of activity), or to suffocate.*[30]

What is the seed choked out by? How does it happen, and can we guard against it? Over the next few days, we will look at how what we want can choke the Word and make it unfruitful in our lives.

40. In crowded soil, there is too much competition for nutrients for the seed to bear fruit. Our priorities are evidenced by what we are willing to spend or invest our time and money into.

    a. What are your top five priorities presently based on how you spend your resources? Ask the Holy Spirit for an honest assessment.

    b. Are your priorities competing with or compelling your love for Jesus? How do you know?

[30] Strong's, G4155, "pnigo," https://www.blueletterbible.org/lang/lexicon/lexicon.cfm?Strongs=G4155&t=NASB.

Talk to God about it:

He: What has God revealed to you about Himself? Praise, thank or tell Him in the space below.

Me: What has He revealed to you about yourself? What do you need Him to give you, forgive you for or deliver you from? Tell Him in the space below.

We: What do you want Him to do in and through your life by the power of His Spirit? Ask Him here.

Day 16: What You Want

Read it:

4 Take delight in the Lord, and he will give you your heart's desires (Ps. 37:4).

32 He who did not spare his own Son but gave him up for us all, how will he not also with him graciously give us all things? (Rom. 8:32).

16 Indeed, we have all received grace upon grace from his fullness (John 1:16).

33 But seek first the kingdom of God and his righteousness, and all these things will be provided for you (Matt. 6:33).

Unpack it:

- Put brackets around the command, underline the promised result and circle what you will be given (Ps. 37:4).
- What does the gift of Jesus tell us about the character of God? (Rom. 8:32).
- Put brackets around the two words that tell what God promises to give us (Rom. 8:32).
- Underline the source of "grace upon grace" (John 1:16). Will this source run dry? How do you know?
- Circle what we are to seek first (Matt. 6:33).
- Underline the promise that follows.

Work it out:

The world shouts loudly: *Take care of yourself, treat yourself, and look out for yourself. You deserve it! Me time. Do what you want.* Self-love and self-care are the trending words of our self-indulgent generation. Is the pursuit of what we want narcissistic or necessary?

Where does what we want fit into following Jesus?

Scripture is pretty clear—following Jesus is characterized by self-denial,[31] being empty of self,[32] and being crucified with Christ.[33] And the two commandments that Jesus highlighted as the greatest are to love God and your neighbour *as yourself.*

[31] Luke 9:23.
[32] Philippians 2:6–8.
[33] Galatians 2:20.

I have often wondered: what am I supposed to do with what I want?

41. Do you believe God cares about the desires of your heart?

    a. Why or why not?

    b. What has influenced this belief?

    c. What might it look like to delight yourself in the Lord?

While the world shouts loudly, it also assumes that *we actually know* how to take care of ourselves. I'm not saying unwinding to a show on Netflix will suffocate our souls, but as one who has gotten to the "Are you still watching?" screen, I know that impulsively pursuing what I think I want ironically is often an empty well of dissatisfaction. We err if we believe that what our souls *truly desire* can be found outside of loving God and others.

If we believe God cares only about necessity but not satisfaction, we will pursue what we want the way we want.

When we fill our hearts, minds, schedules and bucket lists with what we think we want, and pursue them with God-like weight, the result is spiritual suffocation, not satisfaction. When we answer "What about what I want?" with a lie rather than truth, our hearts can turn thorny. These lies often flow from the same root as the original deception in the garden—**that God takes and the world gives.**

But pause for a moment and consider the generosity of our God.

He zipped all His divinity into human flesh to walk in our shoes and carry our sin to pave the way for us to come home. He gives grace upon grace from His everlasting fullness, not from a tank with a limited supply. And He promises to grant our heart's desires when we delight ourselves in Him.

Who do you think cares more about what you want—you, or the One who sent *His own and only Son* to pay with His life so you could have yours?[34]

42. Think about your answer to the above question with gut-level honesty.
    Write it here: ________________

The One who gives grace upon grace from His *fullness* knows a little more about *fulfillment* than us—the ones who have much experience with empty wells.

God promises to supply our every need according to His glorious riches,[35] and to give us our heart's desires if we delight ourselves in Him.[36] If what we want will not lead to life, God loves us enough to change our desires until they're aligned with His, and thus, give us life.

Are you willing to believe that the answers to "What about me?" and "What about what I want?" are ultimately satisfied in Him, as you seek Him first? Will you believe losing yourself in God is the real way to love yourself?

At the end of the day, we often find a way to do what we want.

This is why I began praying that He would change what I want. I asked Him to flood out my desires for lesser things with a greater desire to know and love Him. The flourishing life, where my needs are met and my desires are satisfied, is exclusively available in Jesus.

But if we are unwilling to trust Him with our wants, our own desires will eventually crowd out His truth in our hearts. **Want always finds a way.** But remember, the flourishing life is at stake. In spacious soil, a heart has room to seek to know and love God first. This fuels everything else.

No one cares more about what you want than your good Father.

43. What do you **want** right now? Write it in the space below whether it's material, relational or circumstantial, or something else.

[34] Romans 8:32.
[35] Philippians 4:19.
[36] Psalm 37:4.

a. How are you trying to get it?

b. Ask the Holy Spirit to peel back the layers and reveal what belief is attached to it. If you get the thing that you want, what will happen? Keep chasing it down. Then what?

c. Is there a belief that it will bring more security, significance or sufficiency to your life? *Security?* (I'll be more loved.) *Significance?* (I'll be more valuable.) *Sufficiency?* (I'll be/it'll be enough.)

d. How well is it working?

e. Are you willing to believe that the deepest desires of your heart (lasting security, significance and sufficiency) are exclusively available through Christ? What would it look like to make room in your heart by **seeking Him first?**

f. Are you willing to delight yourself in the Lord and trust that He will give you the desires of your heart in His way and in His timing? If so, ask Him to do this:

Make me want You *more than anything*, Lord Jesus.

Talk to God about it:

He: What has God revealed to you about Himself? Praise, thank or tell Him in the space below.

Me: What has He revealed to you about yourself? What do you need Him to give you, forgive you for or deliver you from? Tell Him in the space below.

We: What do you want Him to do in and through your life by the power of His Spirit? Ask Him here.

Day 17: Wants, Weeds and Worries

Read it:

[34] "Be on your guard, so that your minds are not dulled from carousing, drunkenness, and worries of life, or that day will come on you unexpectedly [35] like a trap. For it will come on all who live on the face of the whole earth. [36] But be alert at all times, praying that you may have strength to escape all these things that are going to take place and to stand before the Son of Man" (Luke 21:34–36).

Unpack it:

- Underline the first four-word instruction given (Luke 21:34).
- Circle the word that describes what carousing, drunkenness, and worry do to our minds (Luke 21:34).
- Put brackets around the way that day of being dulled will come on you (Luke 21:34–35).
- What are we to do instead of being dulled and how are we to accomplish it? Underline it (Luke 21:36).
- What are we all going to have to do one day? (Luke 21:36).

Work it out:

My first coffee-making contraption was a combination coffee/espresso maker. It was great until the best of both worlds turned out to be too large for my small kitchen. I opted for a simple 12-cup drip pot that satisfied my caffeine cravings in half the counter space. But then the Keurig appeared on the scene. Why brew a whole pot and reheat old coffee when you could have a single cup, hot and fresh, on demand?

I embraced my very own miniature Tim Hortons drive-through until the pods seemed wasteful, overpriced and, now that you mention it, watered down. The Keurig was out and the Aeropress was in. It alone would satisfy the void weak and wasteful coffee had left in my soul, until I was making coffee for a crowd. The Aeropress process felt unnecessarily long and drawn out, so naturally, I needed a French press. Each contraption left me unsatisfied, worried that there was a better cup of coffee somewhere out there, and I was missing out on it.

44. Describe a time you got what you want and still had dissatisfaction nagging your soul.

One of the primary ways we are distracted from trusting God is worry. Jesus said the worries of this world—the cares and anxieties that distract us and draw us around in many different directions—suffocate seeds of truth in our hearts. **Worry stems from fear that what we want is out of our grasp.**

45. What are you worried about right now? What do you want that you fear you will not get?

The things that distract and draw us around are often not obvious evils. We can be drawn around by trying to satisfy God-given desires in illegitimate ways. **We are distracted if we pursue good things with greater priority than that with which we pursue the God who gives them.**

Distractions compete for our time and attention and are difficult to remove once they've taken root. Distractions can choke out seeds of truth, suffocate fruit growth, and take over if not kept in check. For we cannot chase both empty wells and Living Water at the same time.

Jesus warned us that worries of this world also dull our minds, meaning our minds are weighed down or burdened. It describes the effect of drowsiness or gluttony. **What begins as a distraction can also lull you to spiritual sleep.** If the enemy can't make outright sin look appealing, he will aim for spiritual sleep. If he cannot outright deter you from loving and obeying God, he will aim to distract you with many lesser desires.

What appears harmless can cause us to be fruitless.

Wanting a new coffee contraption is not inherently evil. But if getting the strength of the coffee and the way it's brewed becomes a higher priority than my love for God and love for those I'm actually drinking the coffee with, it has become a distraction.

What worries are distracting you from singleness of heart toward God? Is it having more? Is it having less? Is it having something new? Is it clinging to something old? Is it regrets from the past? Is it having the best? Is it being the best? Is it success?

How are they choking out the flourishing life God designed for you?

46. What worries are presently weighing down your mind? Our hearts and minds have limited space. What has this worry or distraction taken square footage away from?

47. What are you afraid is out of your grasp? How might trusting God with it free your heart from being weighed down?

48. How is the enemy making it appear harmless? Ask the Holy Spirit to shine His light on how that "harmless" thing is keeping you from loving God with the utmost priority.

Will you trust God with what you are worried about?

Worry and distraction are not flies to be swatted at; they're flaming arrows[37] from the evil one that need to be taken down with spiritual weapons.

Have your shield of faith and your sword of the Spirit ready. The Word of God instructs us to capture those fear-based thoughts just like we would an opponent in a schoolyard game of capture the flag. But instead of the casual walk to the game's designated jail, walk them to straight to their Jesus.[38] He has ultimate authority.[39]

You can know God in the midst of worry and distraction if you are willing to come to Him in it and trust Him with it. Experiencing God at this very intersection can lead you down the path of flourishing.

[37] Ephesians 6:16.
[38] 2 Corinthians 10:3–5.
[39] Hebrews 2:14–15, 1 Peter 3:22.

Talk to God about it:

He: What has God revealed to you about Himself? Praise, thank or tell Him in the space below.

Me: What has He revealed to you about yourself? What do you need Him to give you, forgive you for or deliver you from? Tell Him in the space below.

We: What do you want Him to do in and through your life by the power of His Spirit? Ask Him here.

Day 18: Is More Really Better?

Read it:

"Don't wear yourself out to get rich; because you know better, stop! As soon as your eyes fly to it, it disappears, for it makes wings for itself and flies like an eagle to the sky" (Prov. 23:4–5).

Keep your life free from the love of money, and be content with what you have, for he has said, "**I will never leave you nor forsake you**" (Heb. 13:5).

"Keep falsehood and deceitful words far from me. Give me neither poverty nor wealth; feed me with the food I need. Otherwise, I might have too much and deny you, saying, 'Who is the Lord?' or I might have nothing and steal, profaning the name of my God" (Prov. 30:8–9).

Unpack it:

- Underline the word to describe what happens to you in the pursuit of wealth (Prov. 23:4).
- Circle the word that describes the evasiveness of your eyes flying to wealth (Prov. 23:5).
- Put brackets around what we are to keep our lives free from (Heb. 13:5).
- Underline the antidote of being entangled by the love of money (Heb. 13:5).
- Put brackets around God's promise (Heb. 13:5).
- According to the writer of Proverbs, what is the risk of having too much? (Prov. 30:8–9).

Work it out:

As a child, I had everything I needed and remember being fairly happy and content. But there were a few "fancy" toys I silently desired that friends or relatives had—Barbie campers and clothes, play kitchens, electric ride-on cars and outdoor playhouses. These things were shiny, and my toys were simple—blocks, games, puzzles and an inverted watermelon-box-turned-playhouse.

When I became a parent, guess what my kids had to have? Everything I didn't. When we bought my daughter a play kitchen for her birthday, my husband pointed out that I was more excited about the pricey piece of plastic than she was.

Jesus described the deceitfulness of wealth as the competition that chokes the Word in our hearts. "Deceit" is *the act of causing someone to accept as true or valid what is false or invalid, or to be misleading*. It refers to that which gives a false impression, whether by appearance, statement or influence. "Wealth" refers to money and possessions, but also abundance and plenitude.[40]

[40] Strong's, G4149, "ploutos," https://www.blueletterbible.org/lang/lexicon/lexicon.cfm?Strongs=G4149&t=NASB.

What Scripture warns us is that the all-out *pursuit* (not the simple presence) of wealth can distract us from the sufficiency of the presence of God. In Him, we have everything we need. If we think having more will make us more secure, significant or sufficient, we've been misled.

What *is* true about money, possessions, abundance and plenitude? They are not inherently evil. In fact, they can be useful, like any good gift entrusted to us by God. **But if we think their acquisition (not our surrender) is the key to flourishing, we have been deceived.**

Jennie Allen writes, "The enemy promises water, but every time we go to His wells, they are empty."[41]

Although we've heard "less is more," we are often tempted to at least check out the well of more. From a distance, it looks promising and satisfying, but it does not have what we need for the flourishing life.

The result of having more time, talent, possessions, money, or square footage is more management and responsibility, not more security, significance or sufficiency as the enemy would love for us to believe. Jesus said, "*From those who have been given much, much will be demanded.*"

Wearing ourselves out to have *more* of this world can be a joy-stealer, time-killer, and contentment-destroyer. That is probably why the author of the Proverbs pleaded with God to give him neither poverty nor riches but only what he needed.[42]

49. What do you think you need more of right now—whether it be money, time or talent? What do you believe it will provide? Is it true?

50. What do you think you need before you can take your next step of obedience with God? Is it true?

The more our hearts are preoccupied with the things of this world, the less priority we give to staying connected and living dependent on the Word.

[41] Ann Voskamp, http://annvoskamp.com/2017/01/facing-hard-battles-here-youve-got-to-know-the-enemys-secret-strategy.
[42] Proverbs 30:8–9.

The truth is, no matter what you think you need more of—time, money, opportunity, help or giftedness—**there is nothing you need that His grace cannot supply to live the flourishing life God desires for you.**

Talk to God about it:

He: What has God revealed to you about Himself? Praise, thank or tell Him in the space below.

Me: What has He revealed to you about yourself? What do you need Him to give you, forgive you for or deliver you from? Tell Him in the space below.

We: What do you want Him to do in and through your life by the power of His Spirit? Ask Him here.

Day 19: Made for Maturity

Read it:

14 "As for the seed that fell among thorns, these are the ones who, when they have heard, go on their way and are choked with worries, riches, and pleasures of life, and produce no mature fruit" (Luke 8:14).

18 "Others are like seed sown among thorns; these are the ones who hear the word,
19 but the worries of this age, the deceitfulness of wealth, and the desires for other things enter in and choke the word, and it becomes unfruitful" (Mark 4:18–19).

Unpack it:

- Circle the three things that choke out the seed among thorns (Luke 8:14).
- Underline the word to describe the result of the seed among thorns (Luke 8:14).
- Circle the three things that choke the seed sown among thorns according to Mark (Mark 4:18–19).
- What is the result of the seed sown among thorns? (Mark 4:18–19).
- Write out the words that characterize the competition in our hearts.

Work it out:

In my aunt's yard in beautiful British Columbia is a tree I take great delight in. It produces many pounds of cherries each year and, thankfully, we are among those who get to enjoy them.

I remember the year my aunt called to tell me there had been an abundance of spring sunshine and the cherries appeared to be a couple of weeks ahead of schedule. We circled the weekend on our calendar, counted down the days, packed up the van, and headed west prepared to pick the cherries that were supposedly days away from perfection.

However, there was an unexpected change in the weather, which meant that though the cherries were plenty in number, they weren't ripe or ready for picking. The empty-handed drive home was disappointing.

While Matthew and Mark describe the seed sown in the thorny soil as unfruitful, Luke rounds out our understanding by describing it as ***producing no mature fruit.***

The phrase "no mature fruit" means that fruit was growing but did not ripen or come to perfection and maturity. The phrase can describe fruit, pregnant women, or animals bringing their young to maturity, and, interestingly, this is the only use of the phrase in the Bible.[43]

How might you feel if you saw pounds of developing fruit on your cherry tree, knowing it would never ripen for harvest? Or a growing pregnancy, knowing it would not culminate in birth? Or a small child, knowing they would not be brought to maturity? Our hearts ache at the very thought, for we intuitively know this is not the way life was meant to be.

We were made for maturity.

I wonder if we might feel that same ache if, when Jesus tests the quality of our life's work with fire,[44] we see that we did not mature in fruitfulness and productivity the way He intended? Will we see hearts that are hard, shallow, crowded, unwilling?

According to Jesus, the competition that crowds our hearts are things we are all too familiar with—worry, wealth, desire for other things, and pleasures of this life (gratifying the natural or sinful desires, and the natural tendency towards evil things—acting out of fear, pride or guilt).

We don't have to be doing worldly things for our hearts to be crowded; we can simply desire them. The longings don't need to be carried out to crowd the truth; they can simply occupy space in our hearts.

51. Jesus warns us that our desire for other things can choke out the seed of His Word. Describe an "other thing" you've longed for—whether for a season of life, relationship or circumstance. Did it satisfy the way you expected? Why or why not?

How can we know if we are not maturing? Nothing will be hidden from Him when our lives are tested, and nothing is hidden from Him now.

Only God can reveal to us now what competition is crowding out our completion while there is still time for course corrections.

He can show us how our hearts are crowded. We desperately need His living and active Word to judge the thoughts and attitudes of our hearts.[45] We can ask Him to search, know and test our hearts and reveal what way is in us.[46]

[43] Strong's, G5052, "telesphoreo," https://www.blueletterbible.org/lang/lexicon/lexicon.cfm?Strongs=G5052&t=NASB.
[44] 1 Corinthians 3:12–14.
[45] Hebrews 4:12–13.
[46] Psalm 139:23–24.

52. What hesitations do you have about giving God full access to weed out your heart? What lies might your heart still believe that stem from believing that God is a taker, and the world is a giver? Do you believe that His will for you is to flourish?

As we offer Him access to our hearts, He will weed out the desires and pleasures that keep us from flourishing.

Talk to God about it:

He: What has God revealed to you about Himself? Praise, thank or tell Him in the space below.

Me: What has He revealed to you about yourself? What do you need Him to give you, forgive you for or deliver you from? Tell Him in the space below.

We: What do you want Him to do in and through your life by the power of His Spirit? Ask Him here.

Day 20: The Thing About the Thorns

Read it:

8 My Father is glorified by this: that you produce much fruit and prove to be my disciples (John 15:8).

22 But the fruit of the Spirit is love, joy, peace, patience, kindness, goodness,
faithfulness, 23 gentleness, and self-control. The law is not against such things. 24 Now those who
belong to Christ Jesus have crucified the flesh with its passions and desires. 25 If we live by the
Spirit, let us also keep in step with the Spirit (Gal. 5:22–25).

Unpack it:

- What brings glory and to whom? (John 15:8).
- What in our lives is proof that we are disciples of Jesus Christ? (John 15:8).
- Underline the nine characteristics of the fruit of the Spirit (Gal. 5:22–23).
- What have those who belong to Christ done to the passions and desires of the flesh? (Gal. 5:24).

Work it out:

The thing about the thorny ground is—**what *crowds* the soil is *costly***. The seed sown on it was *unfruitful*. The worries, riches and pleasures of this world, like the thorns, grow together with the truth and eventually suffocate it, leaving a choked crop.

What will you desire *most*—the world or the Word?

Are you willing to yield what you want to God? Will you invite and continue allowing Jesus not only to be your Saviour but your ***Lord****—one with undisputed ownership, control and authority*[47] over your *desires*?

If we do not yield our desires to God, we risk unfruitfulness. Our lives will not yield what they ought to.

According to Jesus, the proof that we belong to Him is in the fruit. **What do we do if we look around and don't find fruit?**

[47] Ken Dyck, definition of "Lord" in Freedom Session.

1. **Repent.** This is not a one-time thing for a follower of Jesus. It's the thing we keep doing every time the Holy Spirit reveals inconsistencies between our lives and Scripture. Repentance is the continual turning from sin and self, and turning towards Christ instead to cover our sin, and provide the security, significance and sufficiency our hearts long for. **We cannot produce worthy fruit without repentance.**[48]

Repentance isn't only the only way we initially follow Jesus; it's the way we keep making *more* room for Him.

2. **Believe.** Faith is being sure of what you hope for and certain of what you do not see.[49] Even if you are uncertain about whether or not your heart's deepest desires can be satisfied in Christ alone, a step of faith can still be taken.

The flourishing life begins with a change of belief, not a change of behaviour.

Our belief in Jesus Christ is absolutely supposed to change our behaviour. Our problem is that we often get it out of order. We try so hard to change our behaviour without first repenting of our belief systems. In Christ, we have a brand-new identity as the beloved—called by God, saved by Jesus and sealed by the Spirit.

Belief in this identity will eventually radically change our behaviour. Do you believe that God is who He says He is, and you are who He says you are? How would someone with that belief system behave?

As we put God's Word into practice because we're willing to believe Him, we build a spiritual house on the firm foundation of Jesus. And it can stand firm when the storms of worry, distraction and deceit blow.[50]

What next step will your feet take fuelled by faith?

Perhaps it is choosing to seek the Word before the world because **you believe** God alone holds what you need for the day. It might look like making a simple confession—*even if I achieve* [insert what you want right now], ***I believe*** *that lasting soul satisfaction is only found in You*. Maybe it's not letting go of the things you think will win the approval of others because **you believe** you have the approval of God through Jesus Christ.

[48] Matthew 3:8.
[49] Hebrews 11:6.
[50] Matthew 7:24–28.

53. What kind of competition might be occupying square footage in your heart? What do you want Him to do about it?

Will you ask God to remove the competition so your life may come to completion?

Talk to God about it:

He: What has God revealed to you about Himself? Praise, thank or tell Him in the space below.

Me: What has He revealed to you about yourself? What do you need Him to give you, forgive you for or deliver you from? Tell Him in the space below.

We: What do you want Him to do in and through your life by the power of His Spirit? Ask Him here.

Day 21: Reflect

Look Back at the Thorns:

When you look over the last six days of responses, do you see a theme emerging? Ask the Holy Spirit to highlight what He wants you to remember.

What has God revealed to you about the transforming power of trusting Him with what you want?

Revelation always invites a response. If you are willing, write out a prayer of surrender in response to what God reveals:

Video session 4 is available at http://everydaytruth.ca/flourish

Session 4: Want that Works

Competing desires can ______________ our fruitfulness.

1. God, ______________________ my desires.
    a. Then we must ask: Will this actually _________________?

2. God, teach me to __________________ by _________________what I desire.

    1 Corinthians 1:26–31

3. God, ______________________ my desires if gaining them is ________________.

4. God, ______________________ my desires.

"Increase my delight in you so that my desires start sifting and shifting until they align with the ones you hold tightly in your hand for me. Your desire is to profusely bless me, not withhold from me. You are trustworthy. You will never respond to my full surrender by starving my soul and leaving me empty. Give me the wants you want because anything less will rob me."

—Beth Moore, *Audacious*

Session 4 Reflection/Discussion Questions:

1. What has God been revealing to you about the desires of your heart and inviting you to trust Him with?

2. What stands between you and receiving by faith in Jesus what you desire most deeply?

3. What reservations do you have about asking God to remove your desires if gaining them might be poison?

4. Will you allow God to reorder your desires this week? Believing that "all these things will be added to you," what might you seeking Him first look like this next week? What encouragement will you need from the Holy Spirit and others to walk faithfully in that? Ask for it right now.

The Good Soil

Day 22: My One Defence

Read it:

[8] Still other seed fell on good ground; when it grew up, it produced fruit: a hundred times what was sown." As he said this, he called out, "Let anyone who has ears to hear listen.... [15] But the seed in the good ground—these are the ones who, having heard the word with an honest and good heart, hold on to it and by enduring, produce fruit (Luke 8:8, 15).

[21] He made the one who did not know sin to be sin for us, so that in him we might become the righteousness of God (2 Cor. 5:21).

Unpack it:

- Circle the three words that describe what happened to the seed once it fell on good ground (Luke 8:8).
- Underline the two words that describe the heart of good soil (Luke 8:15).
- Underline the five words that describe what Jesus (the one who did not know sin) did for us? (Rom. 5:21).
- Put brackets around why He did it and underline the word that specifically describes what we would become (Rom. 5:21).

Work it out:

I was *that* kid. I suspect my youth leader prayed for extra patience and grace before coming to our weekly Bible study. I barraged him with questions like, *"If God loves us anyway, why does it matter how we live?"*

Today, I know it matters how I live. Choices have consequences, even the seemingly small decisions to obey God or not. But can sin ever really be small?

In Christ, we are no longer enslaved by sin, but we can still be entangled by it.

Physical soil must be free from chemicals or toxins to be an environment where seeds can grow. Our hearts too must be free from harmful toxins, or sin if we want seeds not just to grow, but flourish.

54. In what circumstances do you find yourself the most easily entangled by sin? Which struggles have been the most difficult to experience freedom in?

Jesus said the one who hears the Word with ***an honest and good heart***, who holds on and endures, is the one who bears fruit. How can our hearts be honest when Scripture also tells us that, apart from Christ Jesus, they're full of deceit, desperately sick, weak and frail?[51] On our own, all that makes up our hearts—our thoughts, reasoning, judgements, understanding, and affections[52]—are anything but honest.

In Ephesians 6, Paul lists the armour of God we must put on if we are to be strong in the Lord and stand firm in the spiritual battle we face.[53] Interestingly, the piece of armour positioned to protect the heart is the breastplate of righteousness. Righteousness is our only defence against our once-deceitful hearts.

This righteousness is twofold. Through Christ, we have right standing with God. When we believed in Him and received Him as Lord and Saviour, we entered into the great exchange, our sinful lives for His spotless one. In theological terms, this is called ***imputed righteousness.*** This is a pure gift of *grace* received in *faith* from God who knew we would never make it back home to Him on our own.

Right living aligns our behaviour with our right standing. It guards our hearts from the deception of sin. This ***practical righteousness*** is the fruit of believing Christ's imputed righteousness. But when we cling to sin, we poke holes in our breastplate, invite deception and kill our intimacy with God.

When we are unarmoured, we are an easy target for the enemy. He wants us convinced that when we fail to live right, we have lost our right standing before God. But our right standing with God is secured by faith in Jesus Christ, not our track record.

Jesus not only secured our standing with God but also continuously frees our hearts from harmful toxins sin infects us with. He can align our behavior with our identity. When He reveals truth or convicts of us, we can repent and receive what He's already accomplished on our behalf, however many times needed.

55. How has God reminded you that you've already received Christ's righteousness when you find yourself trying to achieve it?

[51] Jeremiah 17:9

[52] Strong's, G2588, "kardia," https://www.blueletterbible.org/lang/lexicon/lexicon.cfm?Strongs=G2588&t=KJV.

[53] Ephesians 6:14–18.

56. What "chemicals" or "toxins" might God want to remove from the soil of your heart so your behavior is consistent with your belief system? What attitudes, beliefs, words or habits are inconsistent with your identity as a child of God?

Talk to God about it:

He: What has God revealed to you about Himself? Praise, thank or tell Him in the space below.

Me: What has He revealed to you about yourself? What do you need Him to give you, forgive you for or deliver you from? Tell Him in the space below.

We: What do you want Him to do in and through your life by the power of His Spirit? Ask Him here.

Day 23: Fast or Far?

Read it:

8 "Still other seed fell on good ground; when it grew up, it produced fruit: a hundred times what was sown." As he said this, he called out, "Let anyone who has ears to hear listen" (Luke 8:8).

15 "But the seed in the good ground—these are the ones who, having heard the word with an honest and good heart, hold on to it and by enduring, produce fruit" (Luke 8:15).

Unpack it:

- Put brackets around the two responses of the heart of good soil (Luke 8:15).

Work it out:

I've done a lot of metaphorical sprinting. In the past, my often-packed schedule required me to go hard followed by a period of catch up. However, as I've learned the hard way, my current season of life—the season where little human alarm clocks wake up at the same early hour every day—doesn't allow for binge rest.

In *Fiercehearted*, Holley Gerth challenged me to re-examine my preferred pace:

> Today, you can go farther, or faster, but you cannot do both.... ***Sprinting is doable; it is not sustainable***.... Live and work like you're going the distance. This means intentionally choosing a different pace.[54]

We've seen a progression of what the seed can produce—no crop on the path, a withered crop on the rocks, and a choked crop among the thorns. **Some of the seeds showed promise, but ultimately, none fulfilled their purpose to bear fruit.**

57. In your life, what is doable but not sustainable? Is there anything you need to quit so you can run a marathon with the Word rather than a sprint?

[54] Holley Gerth, *Fiercehearted: Live Fully, Love Bravely* (Grand Rapids: Revell, 2017).

Jesus described seed in good ground as those who ***hold on*** to the Word and ***endure in the Word***[55]. A heart of good soil can stick with Him through circumstances.

The phrase, **"hold on"** (translated from the Greek *katecho*) means "*willing to keep or hold fast spiritually.*"[56] Will you hold on to the Word in the midst of your weaknesses? Will you hold on to the Word with your ways? Will you hold on to the Word with what you want?

Will you hold on to the Word while you wait?

Growth happens in stages and often slowly. Fruit is only produced out of a seed that has grown, and **growing takes time,** and time always involves waiting.

Holding on can look like inviting the Word to have the final say over your decisions, choosing faith when it seems like nothing is changing, or praising and thanking God when in seasons of drought.

58. What are you waiting for right now? How will you hold onto (remain connected to) the Word in the wait?

Will you hold on to the Word when it's hard?

The word **"endure"** (translated from the Greek *hypomone)* refers to perseverance in circumstances. It describes "the quality of a person who does not swerve from their deliberate purpose and loyalty to faith and piety by even the greatest trials and sufferings."[57]

When your prayers go unanswered, will you keep asking, seeking and knocking while trusting? When circumstances don't change and the storm continues to rage, will you keep clinging to the Anchor? When there is no fruit in your life, will you keep repenting and believing? When you continue to struggle with sin, will you keep believing that you are still defined by your belief in Jesus and not your behaviour?

Holding fast to Jesus is not only "just keep getting back up;" it's also "just keep getting back down."

[55] Luke 8:15.
[56] Strong's, G2192, "echo," https://www.blueletterbible.org/lang/lexicon/lexicon.cfm?strongs=G2192&t=KJV.
[57] Strong's, G5281, "hypomone," https://www.blueletterbible.org/lang/lexicon/lexicon.cfm?Strongs=G5281&t=KJV.

We get down to confess our sin, our need for Him, and to repent of our own ways. He promises to then lift us up.[58] We get down to confess we don't have the endurance in our own flesh, and then we can get back up because we believe that with Christ in us, we can do all things.[59]

Steady on, my friend. Jesus wants our eyes fixed on Him so we can run with endurance the race He has marked out for us.[60]

59. When are you most tempted to drift away from Jesus rather than hold on and endure with Him? (Ask the Holy Spirit in advance to help you hold on the next time you are tempted to let go.)

Talk to God about it:

He: What has God revealed to you about Himself? Praise, thank or tell Him in the space below.

Me: What has He revealed to you about yourself? What do you need Him to give you, forgive you for or deliver you from? Tell Him in the space below.

We: What do you want Him to do in and through your life by the power of His Spirit? Ask Him here.

[58] James 4:10.
[59] Philippians 4:13.
[60] Hebrews 12:1–2.

Day 24: The Graceful Follower

Read it:

20 And those like seed sown on good ground hear the word, welcome it, and produce fruit thirty, sixty, and a hundred times what was sown" (Mark 4:20).

Unpack it:

- Underline the three verbs that describe the seed sown on good ground (Mark 4:20).
- Put brackets around the three crop yields mentioned (Mark 4:20).

Work it out:

When we were engaged, my now-husband surprised me with dance lessons. We joke that the lessons were another round of premarital counselling, surfacing realities that would need refining. When someone who wants to take charge is required to follow, moving in sync is difficult or borderline impossible. It was not uncommon for our teacher to approach us (multiple times in one class) to remind me to let him lead. Apparently, my difficulty with following could be spotted from a distance.

Our dance lessons revealed that my ability to follow needed some serious work.

The word *paradechomai* (translated here: *welcome*) means *to receive or embrace with assent or obedience. For us to receive or embrace the Word with assent means to agree with the Word, especially after thoughtful consideration.*[61] To receive the Word with obedience means to submit to the command of its authority.

Do you let the Word lead you?

60. When are you most tempted to take the lead? Can you be led by the Spirit when you are charging ahead in reactions, decisions and habits?

[61] Strong's, G3858, paradechomai, https://www.blueletterbible.org/lang/lexicon/lexicon.cfm?Strongs=G3858&t=NASB.

To welcome the Word is both to agree with it *and* actually obey it. Perhaps, like me, you've discovered the latter to be more difficult. How do we close the gap that exists between agreeing with the Word and actually obeying it?

When reading the Bible, have you ever experienced words jumping off the page or found something that makes you want to break out your highlighter? What if that was God's invitation to dialogue?

Whatever He's tapping on, stirring, or repeatedly bringing up might be pointing to what He wants to transform.

How do you respond? Begin cooperating by confessing truth. I use the same outline we've been using in our "Talk to God" section that was inspired by the Lord's prayer—**HE, ME** and **WE.**

Our starting point should be what God says about Himself in Scripture, rather than what we think we know about Him. Praise Him for truth you discover about Him (the **HE**) and what He's revealed about Himself in His different names. For example, you can say, *God, you are gracious and compassionate, slow to anger and abounding in love.*[62] Ask for His kingdom (the sphere in which His rule and reign is invited) to come in your heart and life and for His will to be done.

Then, we must ask Him to surface our truth—to break through the hard places in our hearts, remove the rocks, and weed out the thorns. Only the Holy Spirit can convict of sin, so we must ask. We can continually trust Him with our weakness because we believe our sin in its entirety has already been paid for on the cross. **Nothing He reveals can undo what has already been done.**

We are safe to honestly confess our **ME**—to ask for what must be given, confess sin to be forgiven, or ask protection from the evil we need to be delivered from.

Then, we can ask for the **WE**—to be emptied of ourselves to make room for a filling of the Spirit. He empowers us to actually obey the truth and do what it says. As believers, we are to be filled with the Spirit[63]—and God promised to give the Holy Spirit to those who ask.[64]

Without confession, our minds can be informed, but our hearts will not be transformed. We need the cross to continue bridging the gap between what we know and how we live, we must believe His truth against the backdrop of our own.

Then in the power of the Spirit, go and live in obedience in your words, actions, relationships, habits and priorities. And when you miss the mark, confess and repent.

[62] Exodus 34:6
[63] Ephesians 5:17–19.
[64] Luke 11:13.

Good soil is sufficiently tilled, sufficiently deep, has low weed pressure, is free from harmful toxins, and it has sufficient levels of nutrients and good drainage. In the soil of our hearts, welcoming the Word provides the spiritual nourishment we need and the opportunity to be drained of that which has no place in a heart that belongs to Him.

As you continually welcome the Word, you may even find yourself keeping in sync with the Spirit. Remember, He is leading, we are following, and it's a beautiful dance.

61. As you go throughout your day, ask the Holy Spirit to heighten your awareness of His presence and His leading. Be intentional about yielding to His leading at every intersection—responses, decisions or otherwise. At the end of the day, record what it was like to be intentional about keeping in step with the Spirit.

Talk to God about it:

He: What has God revealed to you about Himself? Praise, thank or tell Him in the space below.

Me: What has He revealed to you about yourself? What do you need Him to give you, forgive you for or deliver you from? Tell Him in the space below.

We: What do you want Him to do in and through your life by the power of His Spirit? Ask Him here.

Day 25: Opposites Attract

Read it:

23 But the one sown on the good ground—this is one who hears and understands the word, who does produce fruit and yields: some a hundred, some sixty, some thirty times what was sown" (Matt. 13:23).

Unpack it:

- Underline the three verbs that describe the seed sown on good ground.

Work it out:

I once heard that the average preschooler asks more than 300 questions per day. With three small kids, I field a lot of questions. *Why does Daddy always go to work? Why do you have to wear glasses? Why can't we visit Papa in heaven? Do you know you are still in your pyjamas? How did the baby get in her tummy?*

Some of their questions I answer, but sometimes my response is, "You will have to trust me." Does not answering all their questions make me unloving? No. It simply means I know that the answer is too much for their minds and maturity level to understand.

Perhaps you've run into your own unanswered questions: *How can a good God let bad things happen? Why me? Why this? Why now?*

62. What unanswered questions still linger in your life?

Recall from the beginning of our study that the path is described as the one who *does not understand* the Word.

The word ***syniemi*** means *"to set or bring together; to put the perception with the thing perceived, to set or join together in the mind in a hostile sense of combatants."*[65]

[65] Strong's, G4920, "syniemi," https://www.blueletterbible.org/lang/lexicon/lexicon.cfm?Strongs=G4920&t=NASB.

To be hostile is *to be openly opposed to or resisting.*[66] Interestingly, tension is defined as *a state of latent hostility or opposition.*

In God's kingdom, opposites attract to a point of tension. How can one be strong by becoming weak? How can one be lifted high from getting down low? How do you gain by giving away? How do I embrace both grace and truth? How can I be a wretched sinner but be made white as snow? How can a sovereign God give His creations the freedom to choose?

63. What tensions have you wrestled with personally? What is difficult to understand?

If you want to embrace truth, you must be willing to embrace tension. **Tension requires trust.** Tension reminds us to continue trusting the One who is completely trustworthy.

I regularly tell my children, "Trust and obey, and ask along the way." I continually remind them of the order these instructions must be carried out in. I want to dialogue with them, but I don't want it to distract them from taking a step of obedience. Jesus said, "If we love Him, we will *obey* Him," not "If we love Him, we will *understand* Him."

64. How have you been tempted to change the order of those instructions—to ask and get answers before trusting and obeying?

Will you trust the sufficiency of His presence amid unanswered questions?

A heart of good soil is willing to trust God with unanswered questions because trust in the trustworthy One trumps the present tension you face.

65. What does "trust and obey" look like today? What could be the first small step of obedience in a long direction of faithfulness?

[66] Merriam-Webster, "hostile," https://www.merriam-webster.com/dictionary/hostile.

Talk to God about it:

He: What has God revealed to you about Himself? Praise, thank or tell Him in the space below.

Me: What has He revealed to you about yourself? What do you need Him to give you, forgive you for or deliver you from? Tell Him in the space below.

We: What do you want Him to do in and through your life by the power of His Spirit? Ask Him here.

Day 26: Productive Fruit

Read it:

[22] God blessed them: "Be fruitful, multiply, and fill the waters of the seas, and let the birds multiply on the earth…[29] God also said, "Look, I have given you every seed-bearing plant on the surface of the entire earth and every tree whose fruit contains seed. This will be food for you" (Gen. 1:22–29).

[8] My Father is glorified by this: that you produce much fruit and prove to be my disciples (John 15:8).

[18] Jesus came near and said to them, "All authority has been given to me in heaven and on earth. [19] Go, therefore, and make disciples of all nations, baptizing them in the name of the Father and of the Son and of the Holy Spirit, [20] teaching them to observe everything I have commanded you. And remember, I am with you always, to the end of the age" (Matt. 28:18–20).

Unpack it:

- Put brackets around the first three instructions that God gave to Adam and Eve (Gen. 1:22).
- Underline the two things God gave to Adam and Eve (Gen. 1:29).
- Circle what fruit contains within it (Gen. 1:29). What would it be for them?
- What proves that we are disciples of Jesus? (John 15:8).
- What instruction did Jesus impart to His disciples before departing? (Matt. 28:19).
- What two things characterize discipleship? (Matt. 28:19–20).

Work it out:

The fruit of the Spirit gets a lot of press. And it should. According to Jesus, prolific fruit is proof we belong to Him. The presence of the fruit means connection to the presence of God.

66. What does the fruit in your life say about the strength of your connection to Christ?

For these reasons, fruit should be celebrated. But we cannot forget this simple truth:

Fruit isn't just for celebration; it's also for reproduction.

I wonder if Jesus' statement that prolific fruit is the measure of a disciple and His command to make disciples is the spiritual version of the physical command given to Adam and Eve—*be fruitful and multiply*. While fruit is delicious and enjoyable, it also contains seed. And seed sown in good soil can produce more fruit.

The fruit of the Spirit manifested in and through your life could be the seed God uses to plant His love in someone else's heart. The peace and joy the Spirit exudes through you during hard times might be the seed of His peace planted in someone else's heart to be able to trust God through a storm. The supernatural patience you show your children when yielded to the Spirit could be the seed He uses to plant curiosity in their hearts about the kind of God who could cause a person to respond that way.

The fruit of the Spirit in your life could contain the seed for someone else's faith.

67. Have you ever considered that the fruit the Spirit bears in your life could contain the seed for someone else's faith? Respond to that statement.

Do you believe that God wants to make Himself known *through you*? Do you believe there is someone God has purposed to encounter His grace through *your relationship with them*? Ephesians 2:10 tells us that we are created to walk in the good works that God has prepared in advance for us. Do you believe that some of those good works involve the transformation of other people?

68. How have you experienced God in your life? What personal experiences (in the Word and circumstances) would you draw from if you were asked, *"How do you know God is trustworthy?"*

Before you panic about what it means to make a disciple, consider Jennie Allen's simple definition: *To know and love Jesus and help someone else to do the same.*

69. How can you make known the way God has made Himself known to you? Ask the Holy Spirit for a spiritual conversation this week with someone who needs to know what you know.

Remember, fruit production is never the result of performance but connection. If you had a Gala apple tree in your front yard, the fruit would benefit neighbours, friends, family and even strangers. The tree would produce naturally because of the seed it came from being planted in good soil. In the same way, we don't need to go out and try to produce fruit; we need to welcome Jesus' words found in John 15:5:

"I am the vine; you are the branches. If a man remains in me and I in him, he will bear much fruit; apart from me you can do nothing."

The invitation is to remain in Him—to live our lives connected to Him. The Spirit can yield fruit in any season of our lives if our connection to and dependence on Jesus remains strong.

70. What regular rhythms need to be part of your life to live connected to Jesus?

71. Who has God placed in your life so that you can help them love and follow Him more? (If there isn't an obvious answer, ask the Holy Spirit to bring someone into your life that you can help make a disciple out of.) In the meantime, you can begin by loving whoever crosses your path. When it comes to love, Bob Goff says—*everybody always*.

Talk to God about it:

He: What has God revealed to you about Himself? Praise, thank or tell Him in the space below.

Me: What has He revealed to you about yourself? What do you need Him to give you, forgive you for or deliver you from? Tell Him in the space below.

We: What do you want Him to do in and through your life by the power of His Spirit? Ask Him here.

Day 27: Are You All In?

Read it:

23 But the one sown on the good ground—this is one who hears and understands the word, who does produce fruit and yields: some a hundred, some sixty, some thirty times what was sown (Matt. 13:23).

Unpack it:

- Underline the three kinds of yield from the good soil (Matt. 13:23).

Work it out:

A couple of years ago, I was gifted with the deepest cleaning my house had ever seen. The house was immaculate. We searched, trying to find any dust that was missed, and couldn't find a single speck. We vowed that this would be the time we would turn over a new leaf and keep the house clean.

For approximately three days, we followed the kids around with the broom and put everything away in its proper place after using it. But then our real habits surfaced, and the house began to look like ours again—lived in and in need of a clean.

Apparently, my house doesn't stay clean forever because it gets cleaned once. It stays clean only as we get in the continual habit of putting away what we take out, cleaning what we dirty and getting rid of what we do not need.

72. Describe a season where you thought, "I've got it from here," only to find you still needed Jesus. Thank Him that He is the one carrying to completion the good work He started in you.

Cleaning is a continuous process; so is cultivating a kingdom heart. We do not repent once, read the Word for a season, seek Him first once, and then think it didn't work and our work is done. **The flourishing life results from a continual connection with the Gardener.** Will you give Him an advance **yes** today to meet with Him each day in His Word so He can transform your mind? And when you miss the mark, will you accept His grace and keep making imperfect progress?

Big changes are often planted in the small moments of surrender.

73. What are some small moments of surrender you've experienced this past week—in thought, word or action?

As we continually trust Him with our weakness, ways and wants, seeds of truth are watered. One hundred percent surrender happens in thousands of small decisions to trust Him over a lifetime.

There is no hundredfold yield with Jesus without one hundred percent surrender to Him.

Jesus promises that if we remain in Him, we will bear much fruit—love, joy, peace, patience, kindness, goodness, faithfulness, gentleness and self-control—as proof that we are His disciples. His fruit in us was always meant to multiply to others.

Will you have the courage to ask Him for a heart of good soil that yields a flourishing crop and allow Him to use you to sow life into others?

74. We've studied the many outcomes of the Word being sown into hearts—no crop, a withered crop, a choked crop, a 30-fold crop, a 60-fold crop and a 100-fold crop. Take a moment and ask God, in Jesus' name and by the power of the Holy Spirit, to yield a flourishing spiritual crop in and through your surrendered life:

What is so good about the good soil? A heart of good soil is a kingdom heart. **And a kingdom heart is the environment God uses to affect eternity. It's where flourishing happens.**

Talk to God about it:

He: What has God revealed to you about Himself? Praise, thank or tell Him in the space below.

Me: What has He revealed to you about yourself? What do you need Him to give you, forgive you for or deliver you from? Tell Him in the space below.

We: What do you want Him to do in and through your life by the power of His Spirit? Ask Him here.

Day 28: Reflect

Look Back at the Good Soil

When you look over the last six days of responses, do you see a theme emerging? Ask the Holy Spirit to highlight what He wants you to remember. Summarize what God has been teaching you in 2 to 3 sentences.

Video session 5 is available at http://everydaytruth.ca/flourish

Session 5: Just Do It

To flourish we must move from being ______________________________ by kingdom work to being _______________________ in it.

1. Ask and listen _______________________.

2. Ask and listen _______________________.

3. Stock up on _________________________.

4. Act:

Session 5 Reflection/Discussion Questions:

1. How do you feel about the prospect of your spiritual fruit containing someone else's spiritual seed?

2. How can you take a step towards being involved in kingdom work, rather than simply being inspired by it?

3. Have you ever asked God to show you where He is at work? What was the result?

4. What questions have opened up spiritual conversations in your relationships?

5. What makes you hesitant to act on the Holy Spirit's nudgings? What feels risky about going for it? What might you be missing out on if you don't?

6. Describe something (a product, invention, method or experience) that has recently changed your life. How easy or difficult was it? How does it compare in ease and excitement to talking about Jesus? Pray and ask God to do such a transforming work in you that you're unable to stop telling people about Him.